ANCIENT EARTH JOURNAL

THE LATE JURASSIC

NOTES, DRAWINGS, AND OBSERVATIONS FROM PREHISTORY

BY JUAN CARLOS ALONSO & GREGORY S. PAUL

*For Betty and Dalí, your undying
support and endless inspiration make
everything worthwhile.
Love, Juan Carlos.*

Quarto is the authority on a wide range of topics.
Quarto educates, entertains, and enriches the lives of our readers—
enthusiasts and lovers of hands-on living.
www.quartoknows.com

6 Orchard Road, Suite 100
Lake Forest, CA 92630
quartoknows.com
Visit our blogs @quartoknows.com

Printed in China
1 3 5 7 9 10 8 6 4 2

Table of Contents

Foreword

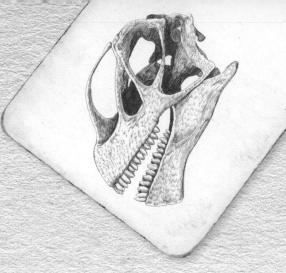

Matthew T. Mossbrucker

Director & Chief Curator

Morrison Natural History Museum, Morrison, Colorado

Jurassic! For kids (and some adults), this word immediately brings to mind images of giant dinosaurs crashing and smashing their way through a dim, primeval forest while a volcano explodes somewhere in the distance. When I was a kid reading dinosaur books like this one, I was surprised to learn that the Jurassic wasn't a where like that imaginary forest, but a when.

The word "Jurassic" refers to a special time in the history of our planet, beginning 201 million years ago and ending about 145 million years ago. Our planet is old—really, really old. The Earth is so old that we use words to tell time instead of clocks. Giving names to periods from Earth's history helps us chart time, similar to how a calendar helps us talk about when events happened in the past. "When were you born?" my kids ask me, and I say "May of 1979." When we talk about dinosaurs, they ask "When did Stegosaurus live?" and I say "The Jurassic."

The Jurassic lasted for so long that it is broken up into smaller pieces, kind of like a year is broken down into months. The Jurassic is first divided into three big chunks of time called "Early," "Middle," and "Late." Then it is divided again into even smaller time-chunks with formal names like "Oxfordian," as well as ten others. Fifty-six million years is a long time, and no dinosaur lived for the entire Jurassic period.

Fossils are the remains of living things preserved in stone that was once mud or sand. Dinosaur fossils are only found in specific layers of rock that were deposited as sand and dirt during a small part of the Jurassic. These remains help us learn about what lived during the Jurassic.

Some of the most famous dinosaurs lived during the Late Jurassic. Fossils of the spike-tailed Stegosaurus and the fearsome birdlike Allosaurus are found together in western North America, along with the giant dino-cousins, Apatosaurus and Brontosaurus. Not all dinosaurs lived at the same time or even in the same place. The oldest dinosaurs of the Early Jurassic are remarkable, like the ancestor of Stegosaurus, the armor-studded Scelidosaurus from England.

The first Jurassic dinosaur fossils found were named Megalosaurus in 1824. They were from Middle Jurassic age rocks in England. Megalosaurus fossils helped define what it means to be a dinosaur. Middle Jurassic fossils remain elusive to this day. In fact, modern paleontologists are still discovering new animals and plants from extinct streams and ponds that once offered Jurassic dinosaurs a drink.

As you read this book, think about each dinosaur and what its life might have been like. Take a trip to your library and read as many dinosaur books as you can find. Visit your local museum and learn more about the dinosaurs that might have lived in your own backyard.

5

Introduction

Come along with us on a journey deep into the earth's history, to a time long before the first humans ever existed. A time when giants roamed the earth and reptiles ruled the skies. A time of absolute beauty and extreme danger—this is the Late Jurassic.

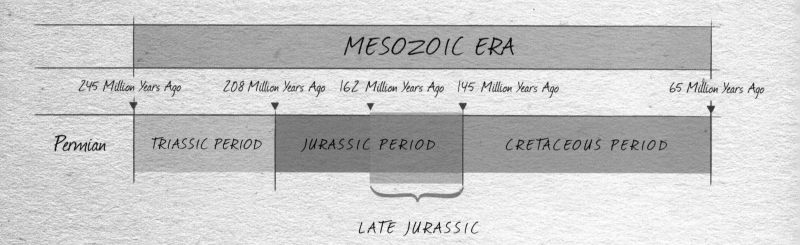

MESOZOIC ERA

245 Million Years Ago   208 Million Years Ago   162 Million Years Ago   145 Million Years Ago   65 Million Years Ago

Permian   TRIASSIC PERIOD   JURASSIC PERIOD   CRETACEOUS PERIOD

LATE JURASSIC

We are now about 150 million years away from the earth as we know it. Standing in lush green surroundings, you take a deep breath and notice how thick the air is with humidity. The unique smell of wet and decomposing plant matter overwhelms you as the sound of insects rings endlessly in your ears. The air is stifling hot, making it exhausting to get around. The Late Jurassic does not welcome visitors.

The Jurassic period is the middle portion of the Mesozoic era, better known as "the age of reptiles." During the latter part of this period, the earth is experiencing significant changes, including volcanic activity due to shifting tectonic plates. The once supercontinent, Pangaea, is now divided into four landmasses consisting of South America and Africa, Western Europe and Asia, Australia and Antarctica, and North America.

The eruptions from volcanoes along with greenhouse gasses are raising temperatures worldwide, several degrees warmer than in modern times. Because of this, there are no polar ice caps, leading to extremely high sea levels. The two largest bodies of water, the Pacific Ocean and the Tethys Ocean, take up 80 percent of the earth's surface, while the Atlantic Ocean is just beginning to appear as a small inland sea. The world is a warm, wet, and tropical place—the perfect environment for plant and animal development.

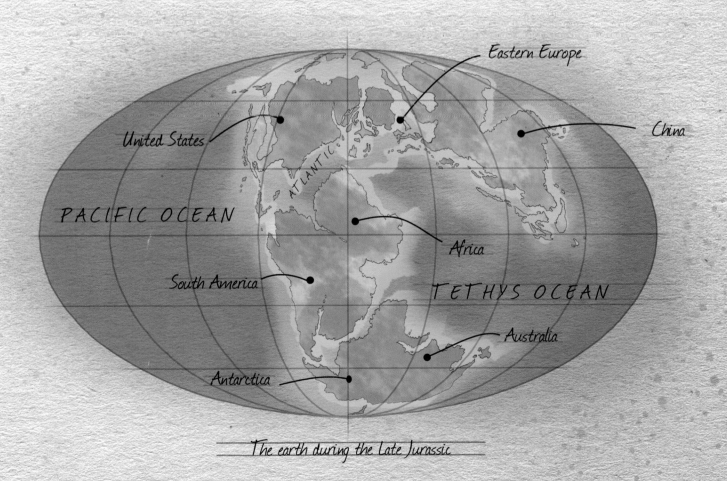

The earth during the Late Jurassic

Around you the landscape is composed of tall conifer trees like the Araucaria (see fig. a) and Ginkgo trees. Low lying club mosses (see fig. b) and Neocalamites, or horsetail plants (see fig. c), stem from and around freshwater ponds and creeks. Ferns and cycads, like Otozamites (see fig. d), dominate as ground cover and low trees. Everywhere you look you are surrounded by greenery. This greenery fuels the growth of enormous plant-eating dinosaurs.

Some dinosaur species are rapidly evolving larger in a race to outgrow the predators that feed on them, some reaching lengths of over 100 feet. As groups of dinosaurs, such as the sauropods, evolve into larger species, so do their predators. Animals like Allosaurus and Torvosaurus are becoming apex predators reaching over 30 feet in length, armed with weaponry designed to dispatch their prey quickly and efficiently. While some herbivorous dinosaurs are finding safety in size, others are beginning to develop armor or speed as a way to elude the jaws of predators.

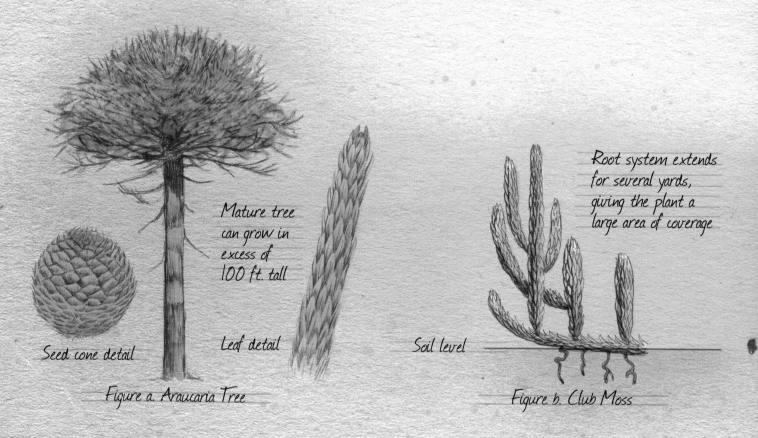

Mature tree can grow in excess of 100 ft. tall

Root system extends for several yards, giving the plant a large area of coverage

Seed cone detail

Leaf detail

Soil level

Figure a. Araucaria Tree

Figure b. Club Moss

Danger comes in all sizes, as smaller predators are filling evolutionary niches and becoming specialized hunters. Gliding through the air from trees is becoming a new means of hunting for the smaller theropod dinosaurs. This method will soon give rise to the first true birds. But for now, pterosaurs, or "flying reptiles," are the undisputed rulers of the sky. Though diminutive in size, their adaptations and ability for flight are unmatched by any other vertebrates.

Continue along on our journey as we dive deeper into the wildlife of the Late Jurassic than ever before, coming face to face with everything from early mammals to super predators. In this book, you will discover how some dinosaurs developed techniques for hunting while others used new adaptations for self-defense. Page by page, you'll see a first-hand, intimate account of what it was like to stand ankle-high next to the largest group of animals to walk the earth. These animals towered over our closest relatives—the early mammals—as they began to stake their claim in a world dominated by dinosaurs. This is the Late Jurassic as never seen before.

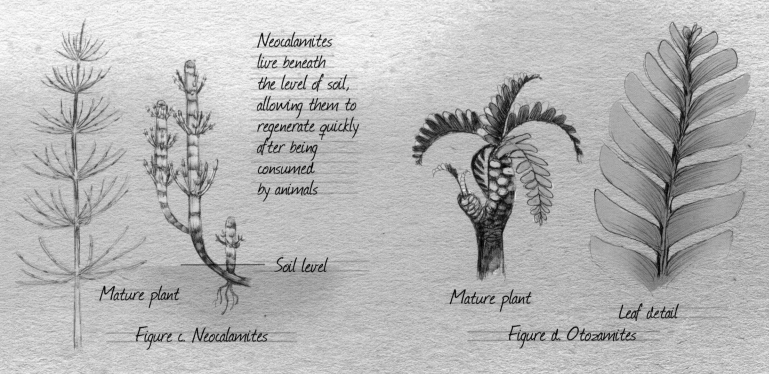

Neocalamites live beneath the level of soil, allowing them to regenerate quickly after being consumed by animals

Soil level

Mature plant

Figure c. Neocalamites

Mature plant

Leaf detail

Figure d. Otozamites

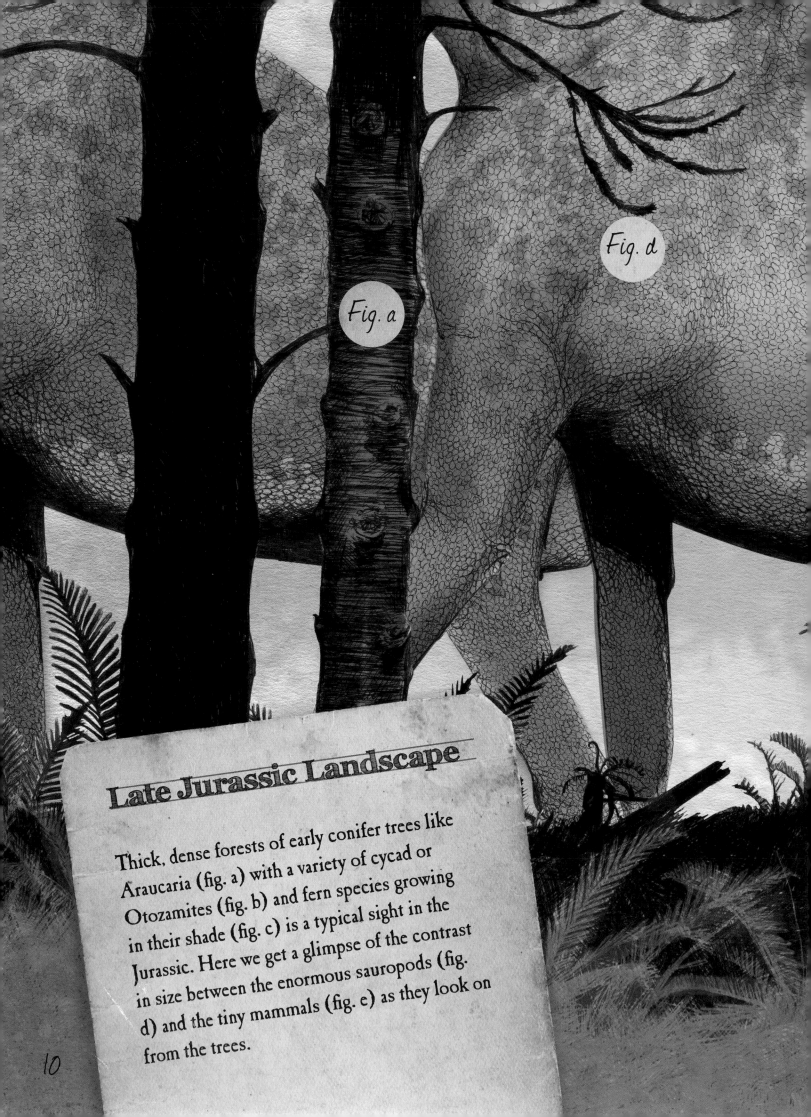

Fig. a

Fig. d

Late Jurassic Landscape

Thick, dense forests of early conifer trees like Araucaria (fig. a) with a variety of cycad or Otozamites (fig. b) and fern species growing in their shade (fig. c) is a typical sight in the Jurassic. Here we get a glimpse of the contrast in size between the enormous sauropods (fig. d) and the tiny mammals (fig. e) as they look on from the trees.

The Theropods

Our journey begins in search of the largest predators to ever walk the earth: the theropods. You find yourself standing on a vast flood plain. The ground is dry, but in a few months, during the rainy season, this area will be submerged underwater. For now, it serves as an open path for both predators and prey to travel freely. Beneath you lies a mosaic of footprints, including small and large three-toed impressions. The largest of these footprints is 1.5 feet from toe to heel. This, without a doubt, belongs to a large theropod. It is freshly made.

The cold feeling of fear runs through you as you realize the dinosaur could be anywhere. Without thinking twice, you begin to run for cover toward the nearest cluster of trees. You can feel its presence behind you, but cannot force yourself to turn around. Within the relative safety of the trees, you keep running toward the densest part of the woods, where you hope it cannot follow you. From the shelter of a thick trunk, you slowly turn to see your pursuer.

9 feet

6 feet

3 feet

Standing around 10 feet tall, with its head hung low to avoid detection, the theropod gradually cocks its head to one side to get a better look at you. It raises its snout and sniffs the air. The look in its eye, one of focus and determination, reminds you of a bird of prey. There is no question: You are being hunted. With small horns above its eyes and dagger-sized, hooked claws hanging from its thick arms, this animal instills the kind of fear no other living animal can. You can feel your heartbeat through your chest as it cautiously steps closer and again sniffs the air. It doesn't recognize your scent, and it doesn't know what to make of you. With a loud snort, it turns its back and calmly walks away as its long tail follows. You have just survived an encounter with a Late Jurassic theropod.

In 1841, when Sir Richard Owen coined the term *dinosaur*, meaning "terrible lizard," he must have had theropods in mind. Theropods were a group of dinosaurs that included some of the largest and most fearsome carnivorous animals to ever exist. Though some were truly scary, in reality, many were no larger than a turkey.

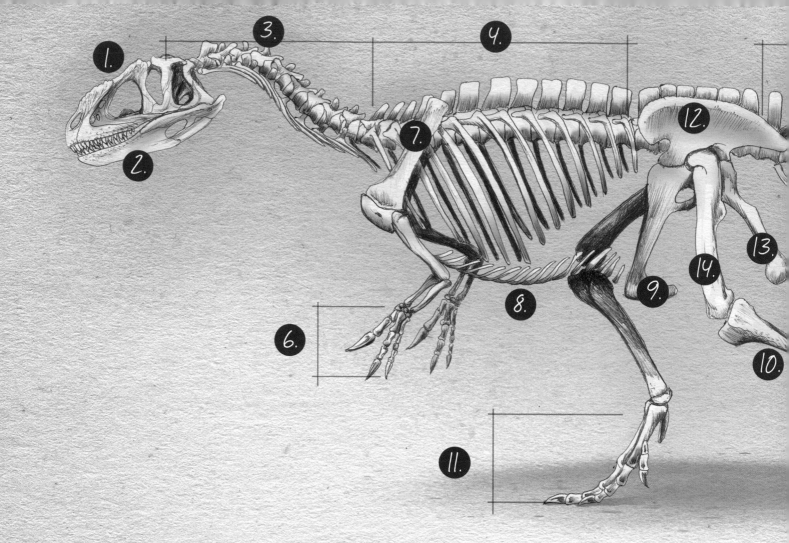

Theropods were a very diverse group of animals known for being bipedal, meaning they used two legs for walking, and most were known for being carnivorous. Some theropods developed instincts for caring for their young and finding mates, much like birds do today. As a matter of fact, theropod dinosaurs have not technically become extinct, as some evolved into modern birds.

Theropods of the Late Jurassic

By the Late Jurassic, several species of theropods had reached unprecedented size. This trend called "gigantism" was only the beginning. Soon super predators reaching 40 to 55 feet in length began to dominate the earth in the following period: the Cretaceous. But in the Jurassic, 30- to 35-foot-long theropods were at the top of the food chain. Many of them had hands built like the talons of an eagle, with a razor-sharp thumb claw over 9 inches long. Because prey animals were becoming larger, some theropods may have developed hunting techniques such as pack hunting, where several individuals worked together to bring down larger prey.

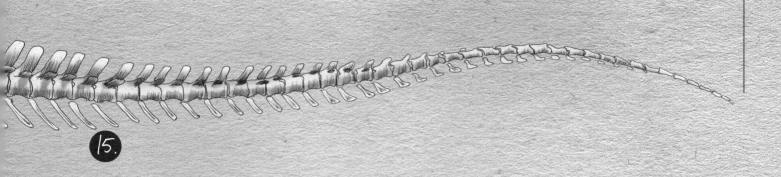

15.

Anatomy of a Late Jurassic theropod skeleton

1. skull	6. manus	11. pes
2. mandible	7. scapula	12. ilium
3. cervical vertebrae	8. gastralia	13. ischium
4. dorsal vertebrae	9. pubis	14. femur
5. caudal vertebrae	10. tibia and fibula	15. chevrons

The smaller theropods were making their mark as well. Species like Archaeopteryx lithographica and Yi qi developed an ingenious method of hunting for food. By gliding down from trees, they captured prey unreachable by any other means, as well as evaded predators. They were the first airborne dinosaurs. Later as these species evolved to become skilled fliers, they led the way to the first true birds. Other species like Ornitholestes hermanni and Guanlong wucaii were carving out a place of their own between both giant and small hunters. Swift and agile, they were proficient at running down prey generally too large for the small theropods, as well as the smaller theropods themselves.

The following pages will bring you closer to the Late Jurassic theropods as you examine the hunting techniques and adaptations developed through millions of years of evolution.

Allosaurus fragilis

Location Observed: Colorado and Utah, United States

Family: Allosauridae

Length: 30 feet (9 meters)

Height: 9.5 feet (3 meters)

Weight: 1.7 tons

Temperament: Aggressive

Coarse, scaly skin

Long, curved neck

Powerful arms with three claws for grasping prey

Narrow, slender built body

Long, strong legs

9 feet

6 feet

3 feet

Allosaurus is one of the largest predators of the Late Jurassic

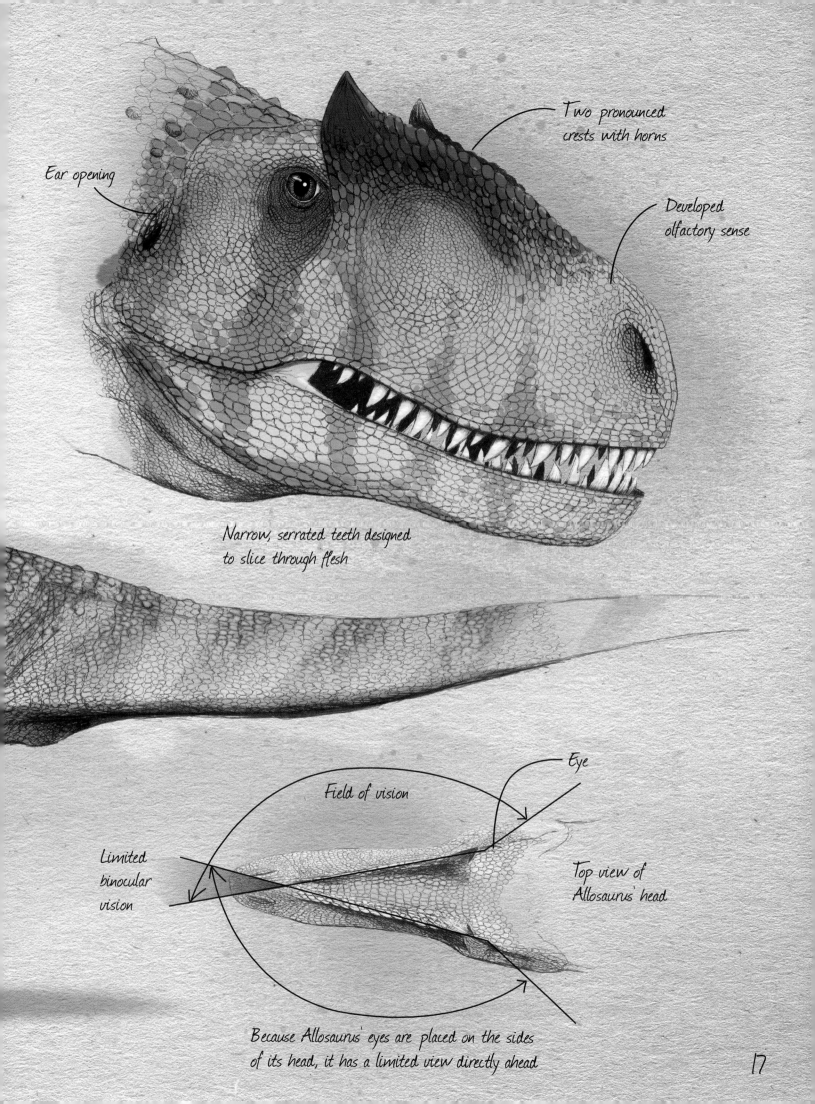

Ear opening

Two pronounced
crests with horns

Developed
olfactory sense

Narrow, serrated teeth designed
to slice through flesh

Eye

Field of vision

Limited
binocular
vision

Top view of
Allosaurus' head

Because Allosaurus' eyes are placed on the sides
of its head, it has a limited view directly ahead

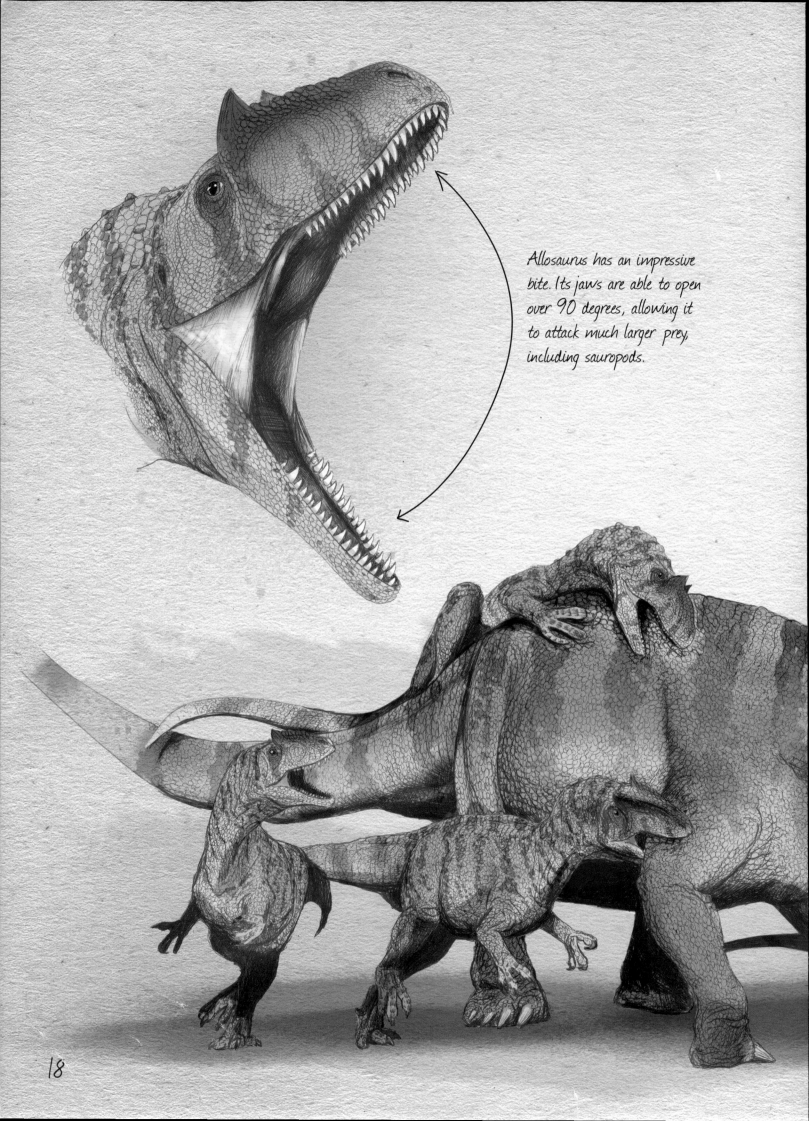

Allosaurus has an impressive bite. Its jaws are able to open over 90 degrees, allowing it to attack much larger prey, including sauropods.

Equally as dangerous as its bite, Allosaurus' forelimbs contain enormous claws used to dispatch prey or act as meat hooks to seize larger animals

9-inch-long thumb claw

A young sauropod falls prey to a pack of Allosaurs. Using its flexible jaws and grasping claws, Allosaurus slows down and eventually brings the sauropod's neck closer to the ground where it can be killed.

Archaeopteryx lithographica

Location Observed: Southern Germany

Family: Archaeopterygidae

Length: 1.7 feet (.5 meter)

Height: 2.3 feet (.7 meter) wingspan

Weight: 1.1 pounds

Temperament: Cautious, curious

Covered in dark feathers

Long, slim neck

Three-clawed wings

Killing claw on second digit

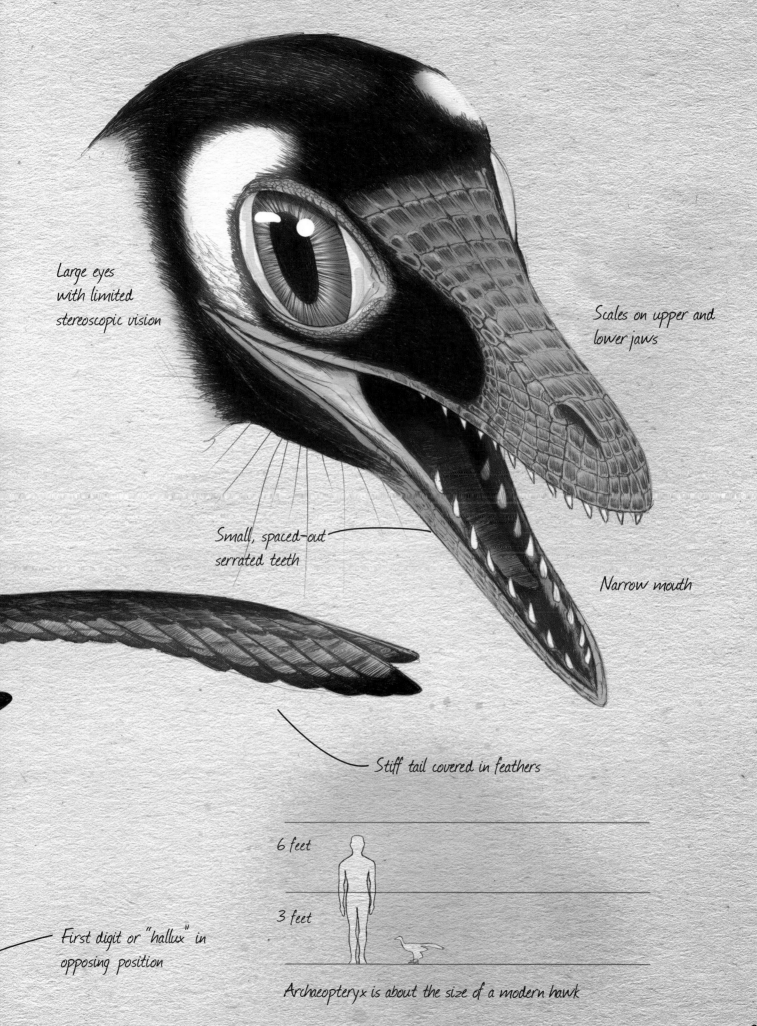

Large eyes
with limited
stereoscopic vision

Scales on upper and
lower jaws

Small, spaced-out
serrated teeth

Narrow mouth

Stiff tail covered in feathers

6 feet

3 feet

First digit or "hallux" in
opposing position

Archaeopteryx is about the size of a modern hawk

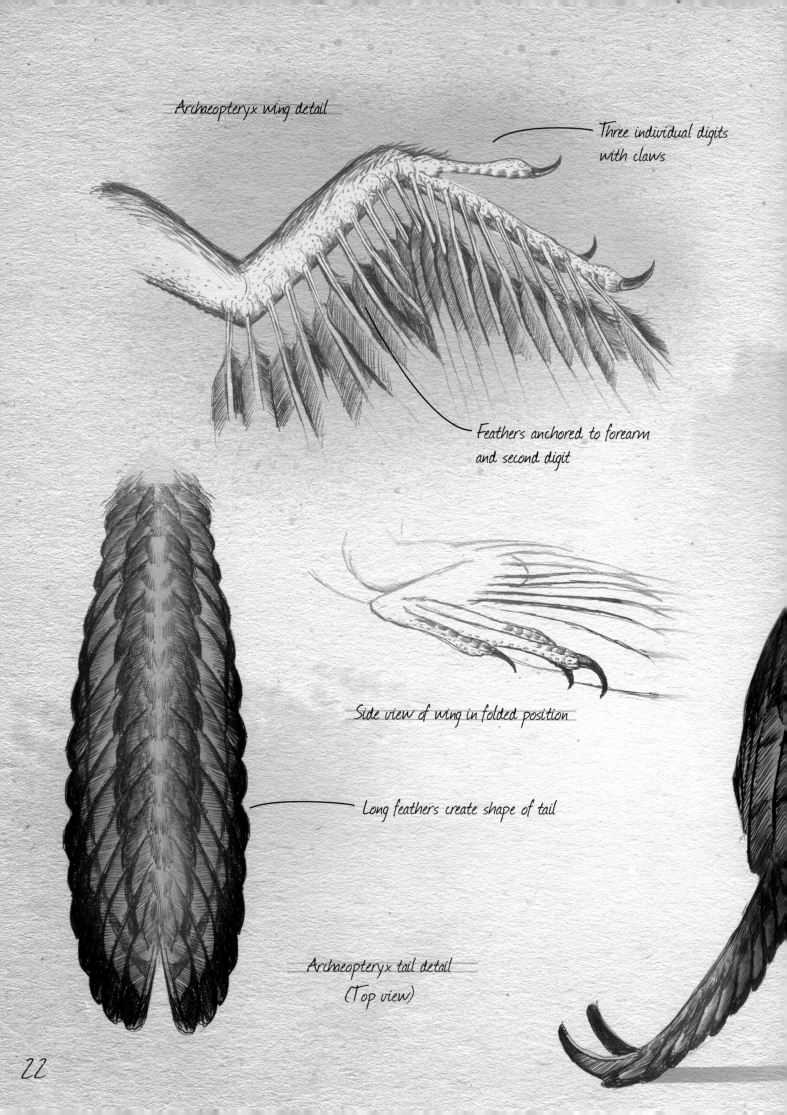

Archaeopteryx wing detail

Three individual digits with claws

Feathers anchored to forearm and second digit

Side view of wing in folded position

Long feathers create shape of tail

Archaeopteryx tail detail
(Top view)

Two Archaeopteryx
fighting over prey

Large, broad wings
with black tips

Archaeopteryx has limited flight capabilities.
It spends most of its time in trees and on
the ground.

Its clawed wings and feet allow
Archaeopteryx to climb trees, then glide
down on prey. It is also an adept runner.

23

Ceratosaurus nasicornis

Location Observed: Colorado and Utah, United States

Family: Ceratosauridae

Length: 20 feet (6 meters)

Height: 7 feet (2 meters)

Weight: 1,300 pounds

Temperament: Extremely aggressive

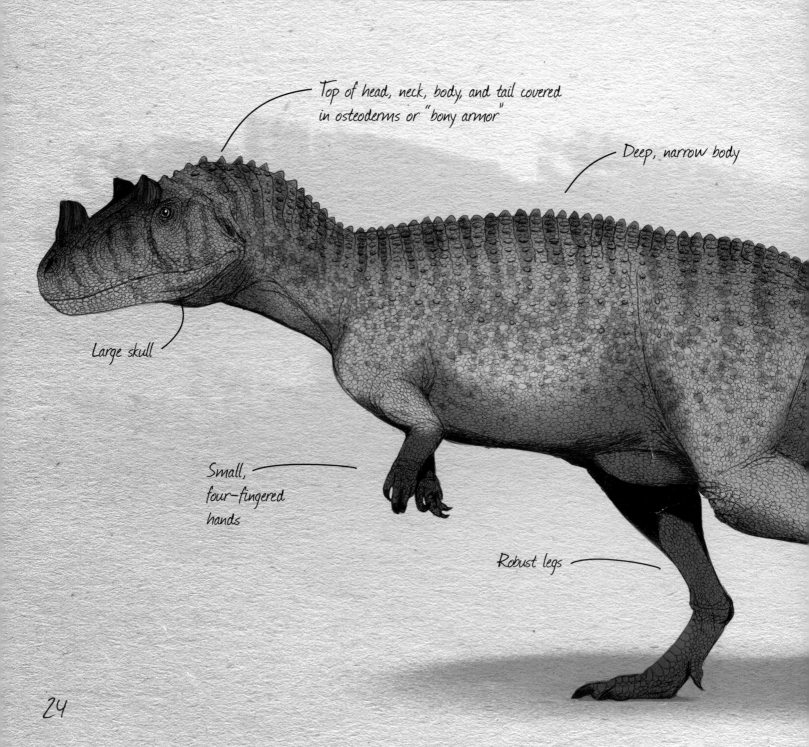

Top of head, neck, body, and tail covered in osteoderms or "bony armor"

Deep, narrow body

Large skull

Small, four-fingered hands

Robust legs

24

Three large horns used as mating display

Small eyes

Very large, flattened teeth

Lightly built jaw

Very deep and narrow tail

6 feet

3 feet

At 20 feet long, Ceratosaurus is considered a medium-sized theropod

Although Ceratosaurus is capable of taking down large prey as well as scavenging for its meals, it hunted primarily by ambush

Here it attacks two unwary Dryosaurus

Ceratosaurus's reduced fourth finger is a remnant of its four-legged ancestors

Sharp claws on three of its fingers

Ceratosaurus left hand detail

Dryosaurus altus are 10-foot-long, plant-eating ornithischians with large hind limbs used for fleeing predators

Compsognathus longipes

Location Observed: Southern Germany and Southern France

Family: Compsognathidae

Length: 4 feet (1.25 meters)

Height: 1 foot (.4 meter)

Weight: 5.5 pounds

Temperament: Shy, elusive

Long, narrow build

Three-clawed forelimbs

Very long, thin legs designed for speed

Relatively large feet

Large eyes placed at the sides of head

Two small crests at the base of snout

Long, slender snout

Long, flexible neck

Most of body covered in small proto-feathers

Long tail makes up half of overall body length

6 feet

3 feet

At 4 feet long, Compsognathus' torso is only 1 foot of its total length

29

Three-clawed hands with a larger thumb claw are used to both hunt and assist in eating small reptiles, fish, and insects

Compsognathus hand detail

Like birds, Compsognathus rests by lying down on its belly with its legs at its sides

Compsognathus hunts the shorelines of lagoons and small bodies of water

Using its small serrated teeth and flexible hands, Compsognathus quickly devours a small water snake

Guanlong wucaii

Location Observed: Xinjiang, China

Family: Proceratosauridae

Length: 11 feet (3.5 meters)

Height: 5 feet (1.5 meters)

Weight: 250 pounds

Temperament: Aggressive, territorial

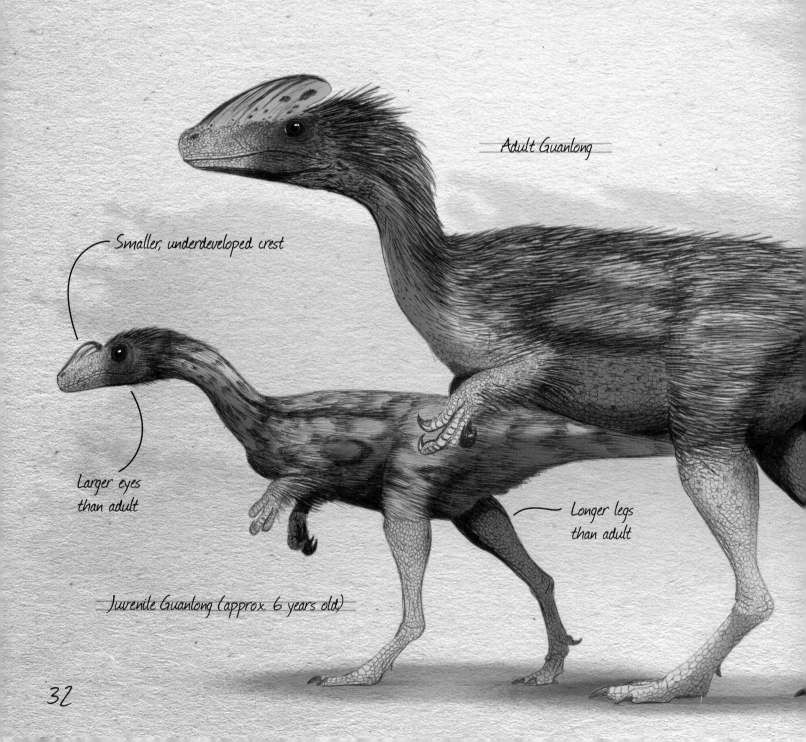

Adult Guanlong

Smaller, underdeveloped crest

Larger eyes than adult

Juvenile Guanlong (approx. 6 years old)

Longer legs than adult

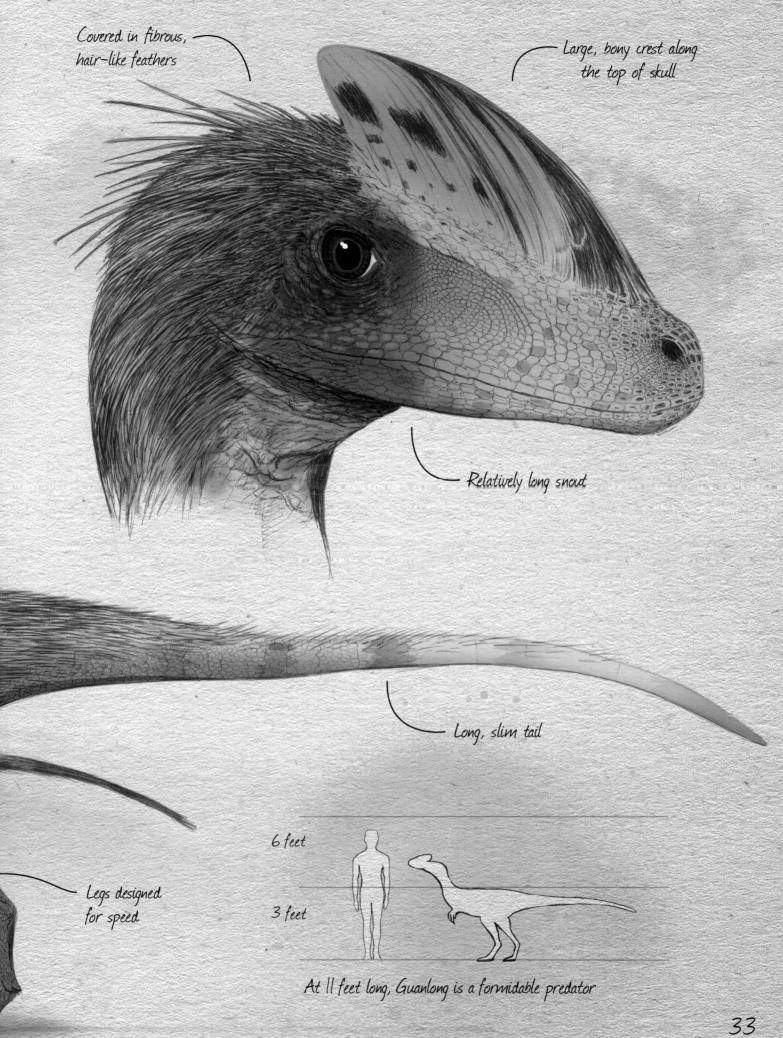

Covered in fibrous, hair-like feathers

Large, bony crest along the top of skull

Relatively long snout

Long, slim tail

Legs designed for speed

6 feet

3 feet

At 11 feet long, Guanlong is a formidable predator

34

A Guanlong parent acts as a vigilant guard for its young. Like modern birds, many theropods care for their offspring by protecting them from predators.

Fights break out during mating season. Male Guanlongs battle for the affection of the females.

Ornitholestes hermanni

Location Observed: Wyoming, United States

Family: Coeluridae

Length: 7 feet (2 meters)

Height: 2 feet (.6 meter)

Weight: 30 pounds

Temperament: Aggressive

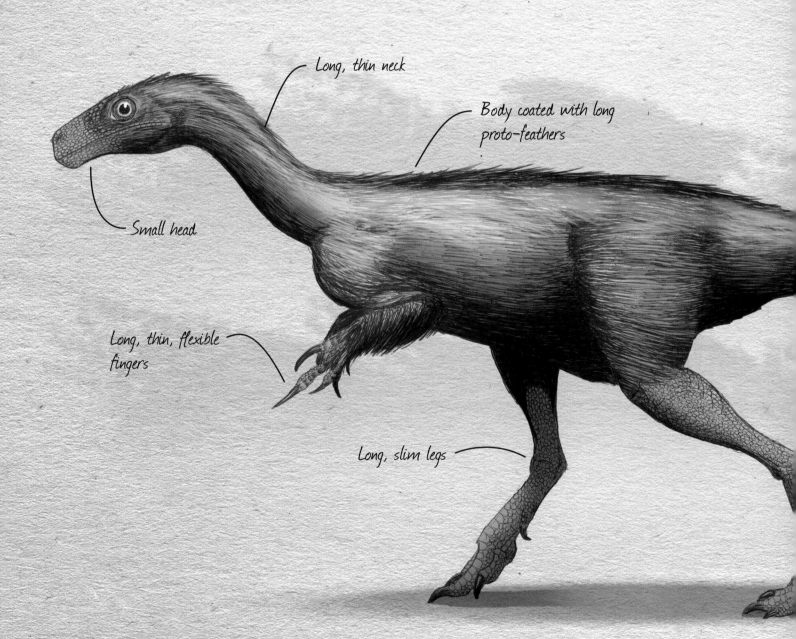

Long, thin neck

Body coated with long proto-feathers

Small head

Long, thin, flexible fingers

Long, slim legs

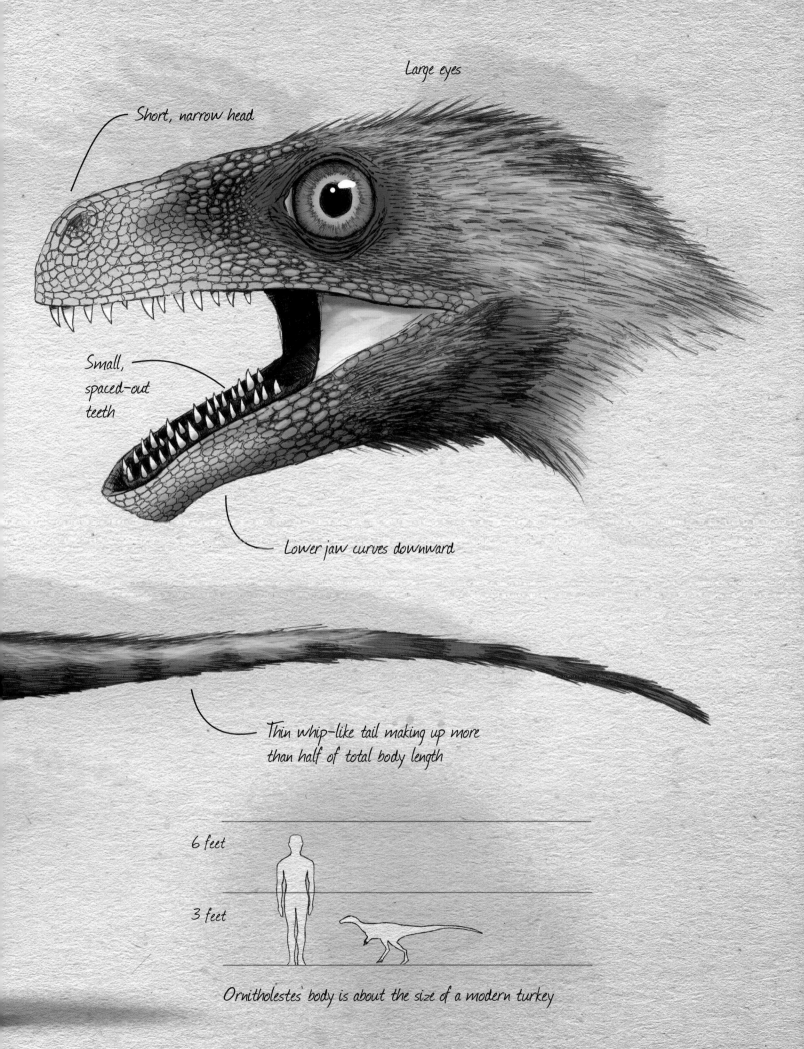

Large eyes

Short, narrow head

Small,
spaced-out
teeth

Lower jaw curves downward

Thin whip-like tail making up more
than half of total body length

6 feet

3 feet

Ornitholestes' body is about the size of a modern turkey

Ornitholestes uses its speed to run down its prey. It feeds mostly on lizards, young dinosaurs, fish, and small mammals.

Ornitholestes catches a Triconodon, an early mammal, and defends it from other predators

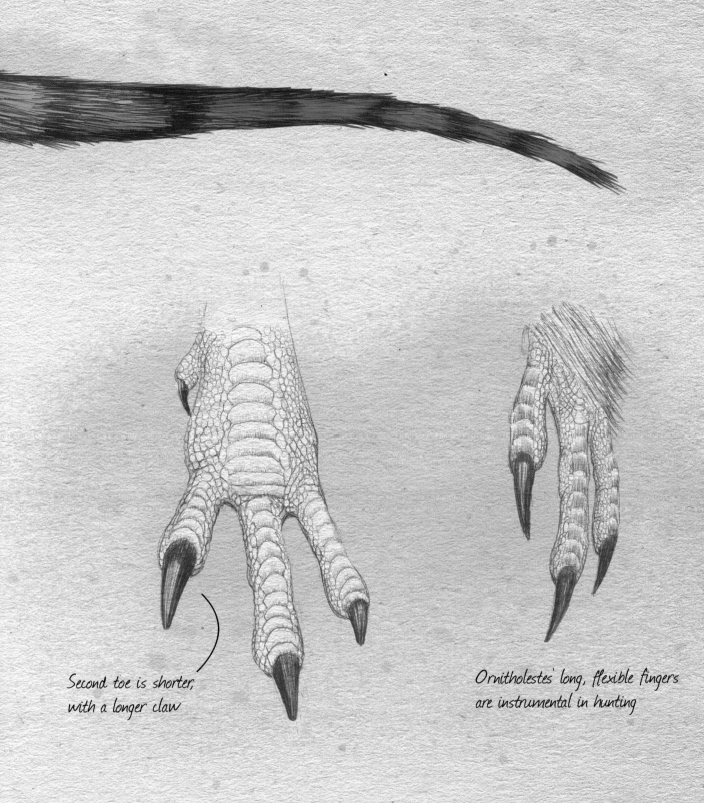

Second toe is shorter,
with a longer claw

Ornitholestes' long, flexible fingers
are instrumental in hunting

Ornitholestes left foot detail

Ornitholestes left hand detail

Torvosaurus tanneri

Location Observed: Colorado, Wyoming, and Utah, United States

Family: Megalosauridae

Length: 33 feet (10 meters)

Height: 9 feet (3 meters)

Weight: 2 tons

Temperament: Extremely aggressive

Dermal spines on head and neck

Long body

Large head

Powerful arms with large thumb claw

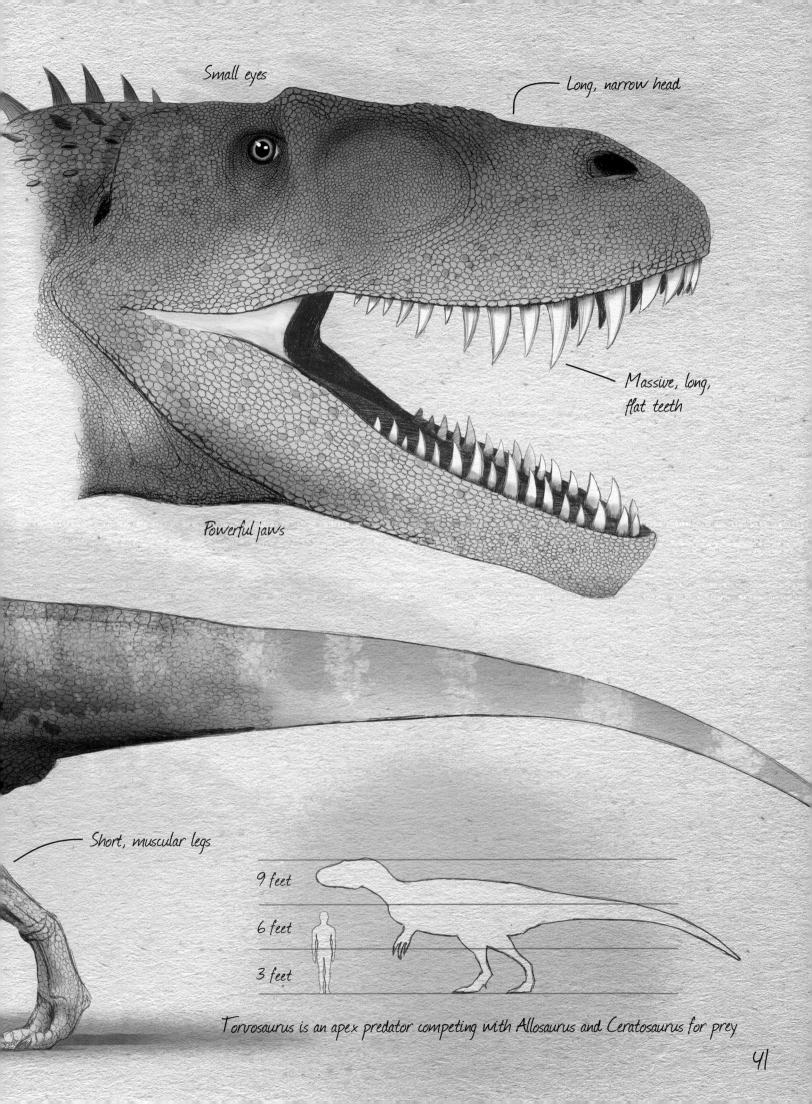

Small eyes

Long, narrow head

Massive, long,
flat teeth

Powerful jaws

Short, muscular legs

9 feet

6 feet

3 feet

Torvosaurus is an apex predator competing with Allosaurus and Ceratosaurus for prey

Thick, muscular neck used to pull large pieces of meat from prey

From the front, Torvosaurus presents a broad profile to intimidate animals challenging it for food

Large feet

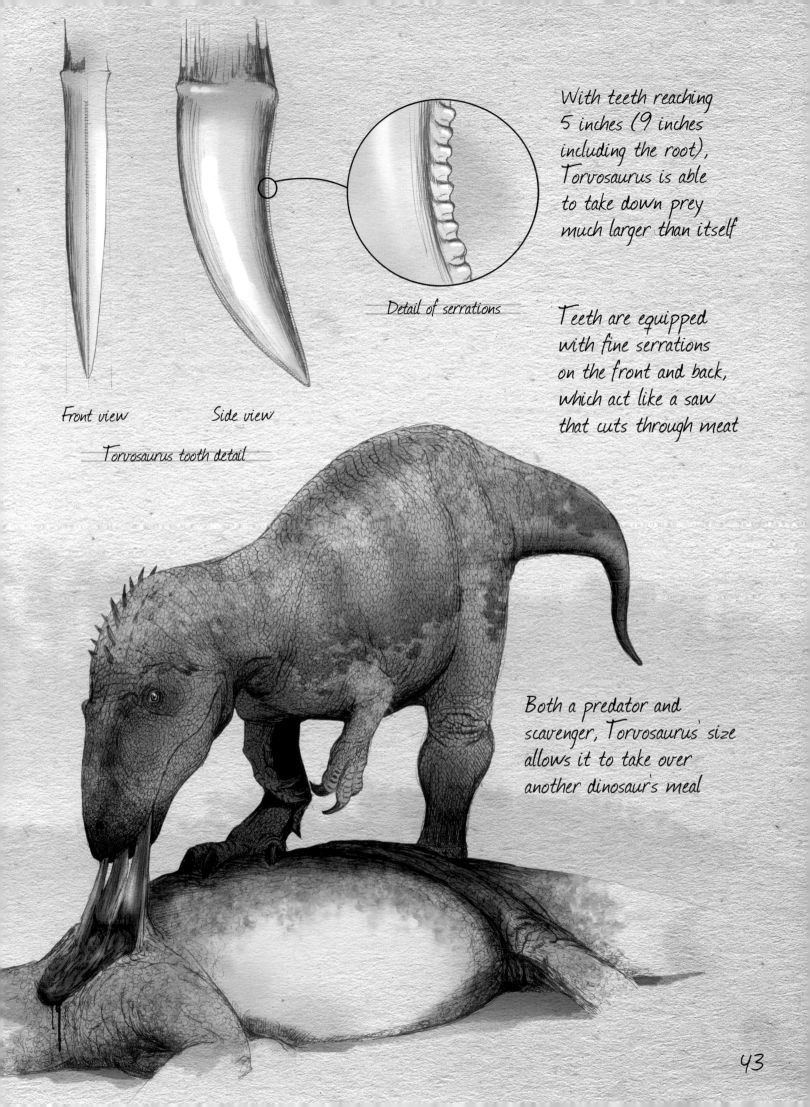

With teeth reaching 5 inches (9 inches including the root), Torvosaurus is able to take down prey much larger than itself

Detail of serrations

Teeth are equipped with fine serrations on the front and back, which act like a saw that cuts through meat

Front view

Side view

Torvosaurus tooth detail

Both a predator and scavenger, Torvosaurus' size allows it to take over another dinosaur's meal

43

Yangchuanosaurus shangyouensis

Location Observed: Yongchuan, China

Family: Metriacanthosauridae

Length: 35 feet (11 meters)

Height: 10 feet (3 meters)

Weight: 3 tons

Temperament: Extremely aggressive

Long, curved neck

Deep, narrow torso

Tall ridge along back

Strong arms with three gripping claws

Long legs designed for running

Two horns just ahead
of eyes

Two well-developed crests
at the front of skull

Deep, narrow skull with
powerful jaws

Long, deep tail

9 feet

6 feet

3 feet

Yangchuanosaurus is one of the largest predators in the Late Jurassic

As one of the largest predators in the Late Jurassic, Yangchuanosaurus hunted large game

A pack of adult Yangchuanosaurus attack a Mamenchisaurus using their claws and powerful bites to bring it closer to the ground where they can kill it

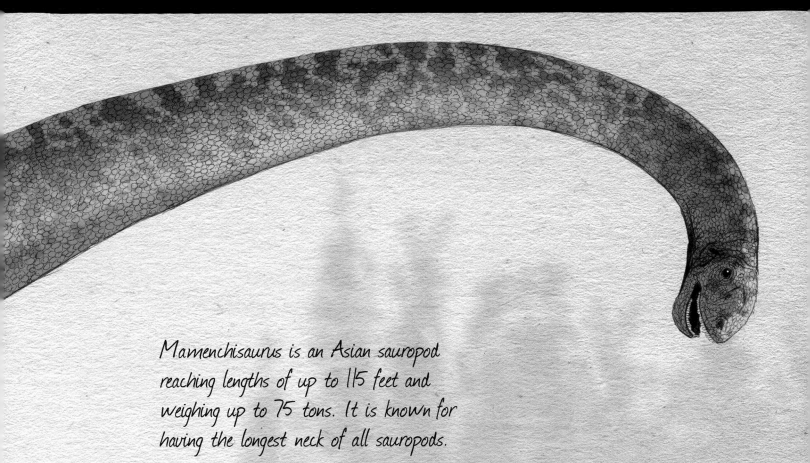

Mamenchisaurus is an Asian sauropod
reaching lengths of up to 115 feet and
weighing up to 75 tons. It is known for
having the longest neck of all sauropods.

Yi qi

Location Observed: Hebei, China

Family: Scansoriopterygidae

Length: 12 inches (.3 meter)

Height: 18 inches (.45 meter) wingspan

Weight: .84 pound

Temperament: Shy, elusive

Short, blunt head

Slender neck

Body covered in fibrous hair-like feathers

Large arms and hands with membrane between fingers

Long legs

3 feet

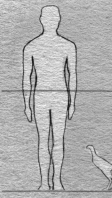

At only 12 inches long, Yi qi is one of the smallest dinosaurs discovered.

48

Plumage on tail used as a display to attract mates

Triangular-shaped head

Large eyes placed on sides of head

Forward-facing teeth on front edge of jaws

Curved lower jaw

49

From tree-borne to airborne, Yi qi takes flight

1. Yi qi is adept at climbing
   trees by using its hands,
   claws, and long arms

2. Once it sees prey, it opens
   its arms and extends the
   membrane to form wings

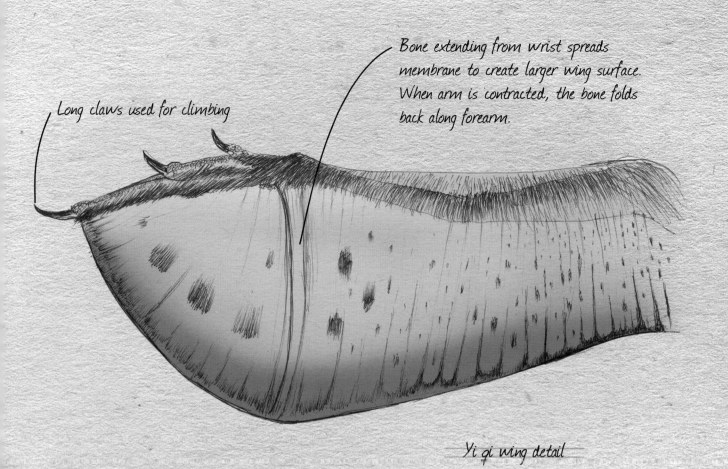

Long claws used for climbing

Bone extending from wrist spreads membrane to create larger wing surface. When arm is contracted, the bone folds back along forearm.

Yi qi wing detail

3. Pushing off the tree with its long legs like a catapult, Yi qi takes flight, gliding towards its prey before landing on the ground or on another tree

The Sauropods

Our journey continues deep into the Late Jurassic to explore the largest land animals ever: the sauropods. Spread before you are vast forests of early pine trees reaching as high as 100 feet above the ground. At your feet are beds of thick green ferns and cycad plants covering the ground like an endless carpet, with intermittent dark tree trunks breaking up the green color. Pterosaurs glide through the air, effortlessly picking up insects without ever breaking their rhythm. It is generally silent with the occasional squawk of a pterosaur and the snap of branches from the trees above. As you look up, a thick neck extends upward, ending in an almost imperceptible head. It forcefully pulls back, breaking another branch. At the base of the neck is a colossal body held up by four pillar-like legs. This animal is so big, it cannot be seen all at once.

It quietly goes about its business as another much heavier and longer animal joins in, turning its attention to the lower plants. It strips the leaves from entire fern plants systematically with its mouth, one at a time, moving its neck from plant to plant while keeping its body still. Others begin to appear through the trees, each oblivious to one another as they continue to feed. You are in the unmistakable company of sauropods.

Sauropods were by far the heaviest and longest land animals to ever exist. They were known for their large, elephant-like bodies with long necks and tails. Though most were gigantic, some species only reached the size of a large bull.

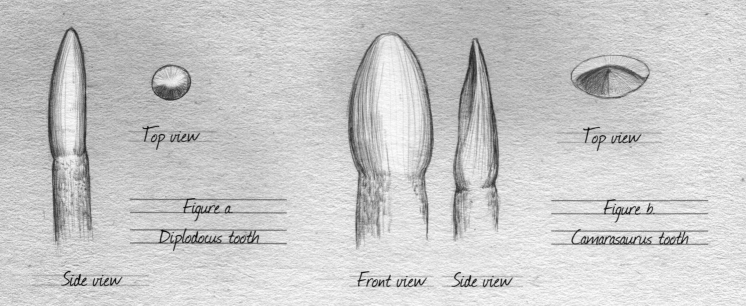

Top view

Figure a.
Diplodocus tooth

Side view

Front view Side view

Top view

Figure b.
Camarasaurus tooth

Regardless of their size, all were designed to be efficient eaters. Some consumed hundreds of pounds of plant matter daily in order to maintain their mass. Sauropod heads were typically small with teeth lining the front edges of their jaws. They did not chew or crush plants with their mouths, but rather swallowed them whole. Their teeth were specialized for two different eating techniques: stripping or tearing. Peg-like teeth (fig. a) were for stripping the leaves from a plant; chiseled teeth (fig. b) were for tearing and cutting leaves and branches. Teeth were shed and replaced as needed every few days to every few months as they wore down.

Sauropods' large, bloated trunks contained fermentation chambers called "caecum," which processed raw plant matter and extracted nutrients starting at the gizzard and continuing all the way through the intestines. Their necks were also instrumental in eating. Most species evolved long necks for either reaching higher-growing plants or covering a large area of low-lying plants without having to move their bodies.

To counterbalance their heavy necks and torsos, sauropods evolved heavy tails. These tails became specialized as well, some becoming defensive weapons with long whips or hammer-like clubs.

Sauropods hatched from eggs and were born precocial, meaning they were fully capable of feeding and walking without assistance from their parents. Nests were usually communal, consisting of many individuals laying eggs in one area. Like modern sea turtles, only a small percentage of sauropod hatchlings survived predation and made it into adulthood. Of the surviving few, juveniles formed groups and eventually herds, seeking safety in numbers.

A newborn Brachiosaurus hatchling makes its way out of its egg and joins others seeking safety

Sauropods of the Late Jurassic

The Late Jurassic is known as "the era of giants." Sauropods evolved and flourished into species more gigantic than the earth has ever or will ever see again. It is during this period that some of the most recognizable dinosaurs, like the Brontosaurus and Diplodocus, live. The Late Jurassic landscape was abundant with herds of great sauropods moving in a constant search for food.

This section explores three basic families of sauropods. First the Diplodocidae, known for their long horizontal bodies, teeth at the front of their mouths, and long whipping tails which made up about half of their overall body length. This group includes species like Brontosaurus louisae and Diplodocus hallorum. Second, the Camarasauridae family, with relatively short upright necks and larger heads, with the nasal opening in their skull ahead of their eyes. This family is represented by its namesake Camarasaurus supremus. And finally, the Brachiosauridae family, best known for their giraffe-like posture, with their forelimbs longer than their hind limbs, causing them to carry their necks vertically. This family is represented by one of the best-studied species: Giraffatitan brancai.

In the following pages, explore these magnificent animals in detail and see their specialized adaptations for both eating and survival.

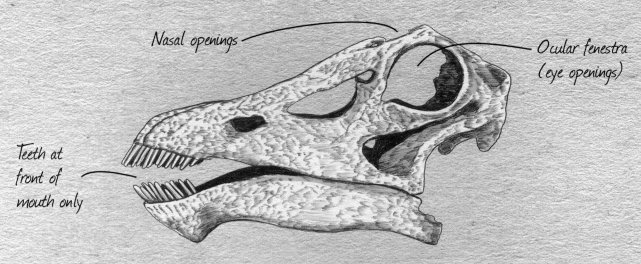

Nasal openings

Ocular fenestra
(eye openings)

Teeth at
front of
mouth only

Diplodocidae family skull (Diplodocus hallorum)

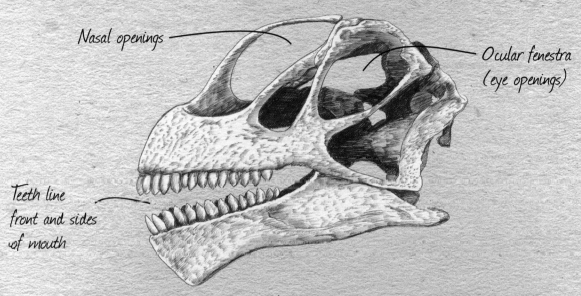

Nasal openings

Ocular fenestra
(eye openings)

Teeth line
front and sides
of mouth

Camarasauridae family skull (Camarasaurus supremus)

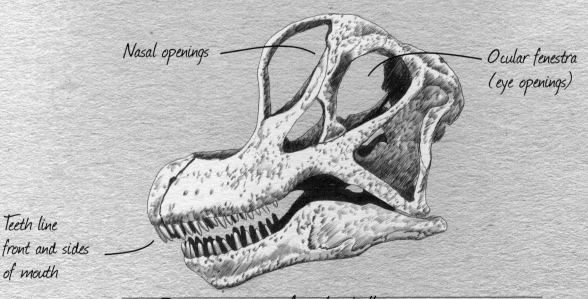

Nasal openings

Ocular fenestra
(eye openings)

Teeth line
front and sides
of mouth

Brachiosauridae family skull (Giraffatitan brancai)

Long, rectangular head

Long, thick, and deep neck

Tall ridge along back

Small eyes

Short forelimbs

Long jaw

Narrow, blunt teeth for
stripping leaves off plants

Brontosaurus louisae

Location Observed: Utah, United States

Family: Diplodocidae

Length: 75 feet (23 meters)

Height: 17 feet (5.2 meters)

Weight: 20 tons

Temperament: Defensive, aggressive

Long tail with whip-like end

Tall, robust hind limbs

9 feet

6 feet

3 feet

For many years, Brontosaurus louisae went by the name Apatosaurus louisae

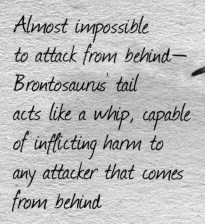

Almost impossible
to attack from behind—
Brontosaurus' tail
acts like a whip, capable
of inflicting harm to
any attacker that comes
from behind

Legs and feet are
directly underneath
the body

The tip of its tail is
capable of reaching speeds
faster than sound, creating
a loud snapping sound like
a whip

Tall neural spines act like a suspension
bridge supporting the neck and tail

Massively built neck

Forefeet are considerably smaller than
hind feet and only contain one toenail

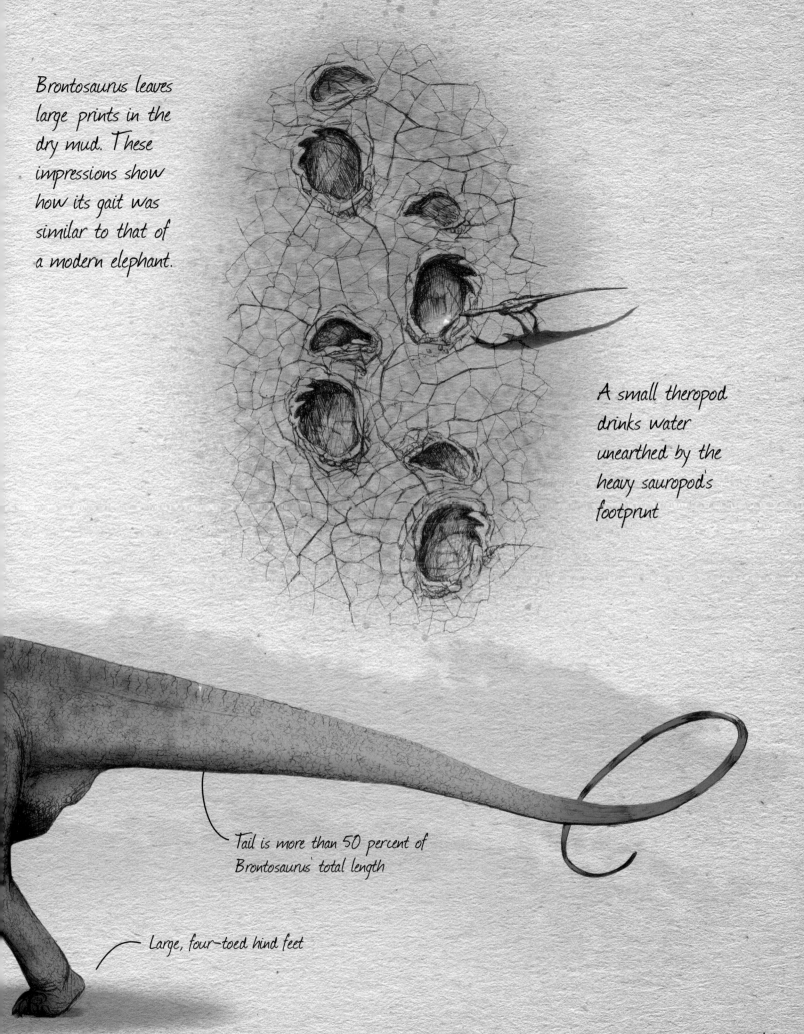

Brontosaurus leaves large prints in the dry mud. These impressions show how its gait was similar to that of a modern elephant.

A small theropod drinks water unearthed by the heavy sauropod's footprint

Tail is more than 50 percent of Brontosaurus' total length

Large, four-toed hind feet

Short, blunt head

Relatively thick,
short neck

Large head for
a sauropod

Tall shoulders

Forelimbs shorter
than hind limbs

Single-toed forefeet

62

Camarasaurus supremus

Location Observed: Colorado, Wyoming, and Utah, United States

Family: Camarasauridae

Length: 50 feet (15 meters)

Height: 17 feet (5.2 meters)

Weight: 15 tons

Temperament: Social, cautious

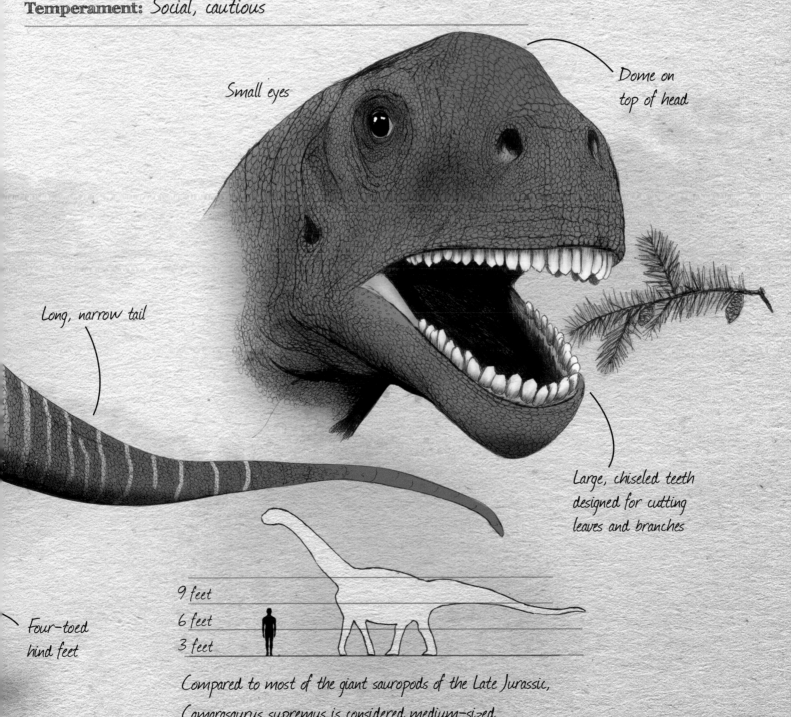

Small eyes

Dome on top of head

Long, narrow tail

Large, chiseled teeth designed for cutting leaves and branches

Four-toed hind feet

9 feet

6 feet

3 feet

Compared to most of the giant sauropods of the Late Jurassic, Camarasaurus supremus is considered medium-sized

Males fighting for dominance—
this behavior is common
in modern horses and other
large prey animals

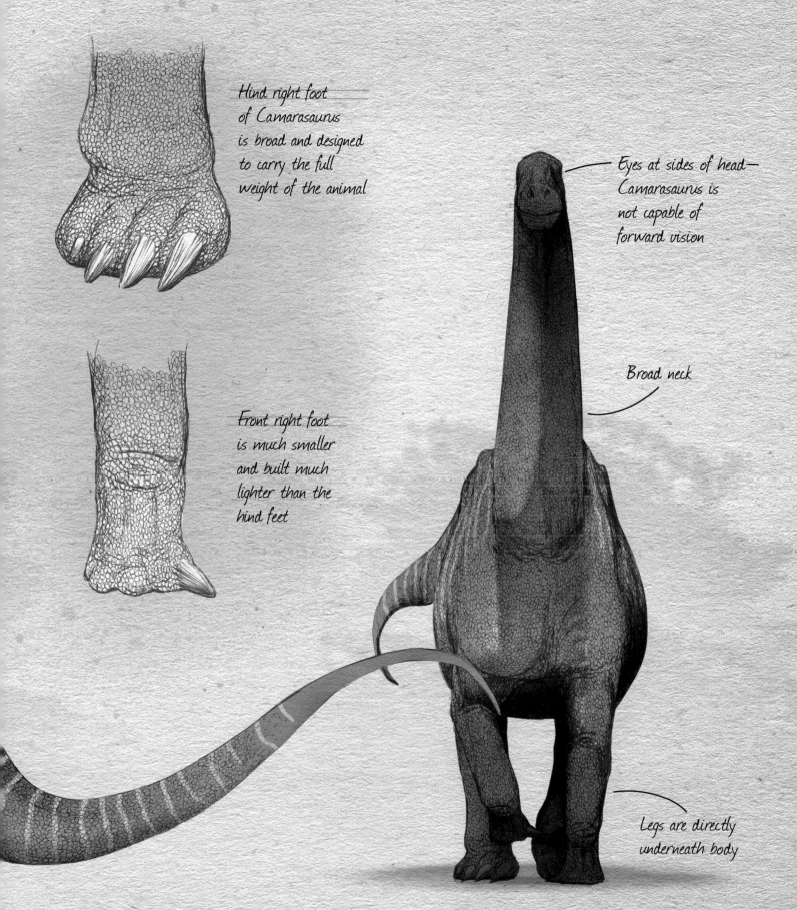

Hind right foot
of Camarasaurus
is broad and designed
to carry the full
weight of the animal

Front right foot
is much smaller
and built much
lighter than the
hind feet

Eyes at sides of head
Camarasaurus is
not capable of
forward vision

Broad neck

Legs are directly
underneath body

Front view of Camarasaurus

9 feet
6 feet
3 feet

Diplodocus is extremely long, but built lighter than most of the other giant sauropods

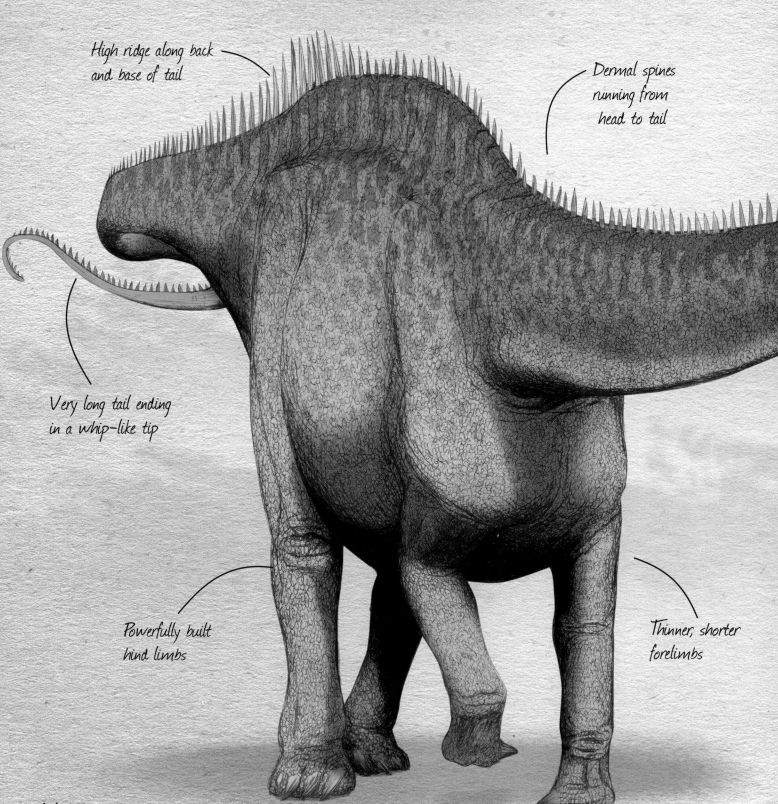

High ridge along back
and base of tail

Dermal spines
running from
head to tail

Very long tail ending
in a whip-like tip

Powerfully built
hind limbs

Thinner, shorter
forelimbs

Diplodocus hallorum

Location Observed: *Colorado and Utah, United States*

Family: *Diplodocidae*

Length: *80 feet (25 meters)*

Height: *20 feet (6 meters)*

Weight: *12 tons*

Temperament: *Social, cautious*

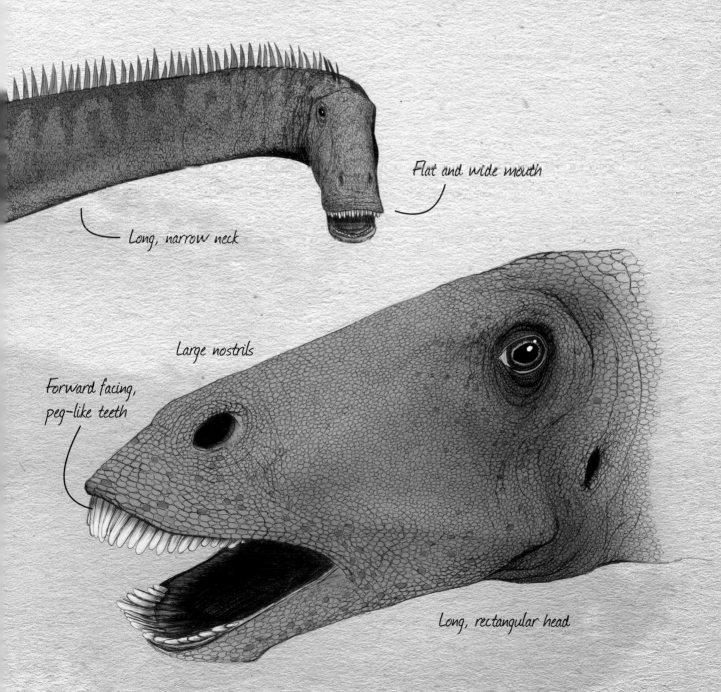

Flat and wide mouth

Long, narrow neck

Large nostrils

Forward facing, peg-like teeth

Long, rectangular head

Using its 40-foot-long muscular tail as a defensive weapon, Diplodocus whips back and forth preventing any attacker from getting close

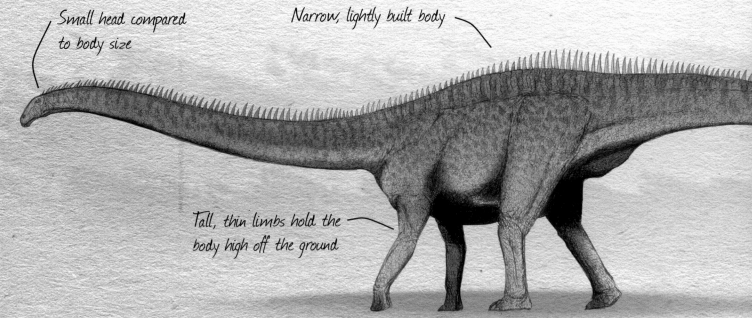

Small head compared to body size

Narrow, lightly built body

Tall, thin limbs hold the body high off the ground

One lash from Diplodocus'
tail can kill or seriously
injure a theropod

Thin, tapered portion of tail
makes up almost half the
tail's length

Tail is more than
50 percent of
overall body length

Giraffatitan brancai

Location Observed: Tanzania, Africa

Family: Brachiosauridae

Length: 75 feet (23 meters)

Height: 50 feet (15 meters)

Weight: 40 tons

Temperament: Defensive, aggressive

9 feet
6 feet
3 feet

For many years, Giraffatitan brancai was known as Brachiosaurus brancai

Back slopes upward

Tail much shorter than neck

Short hind limbs

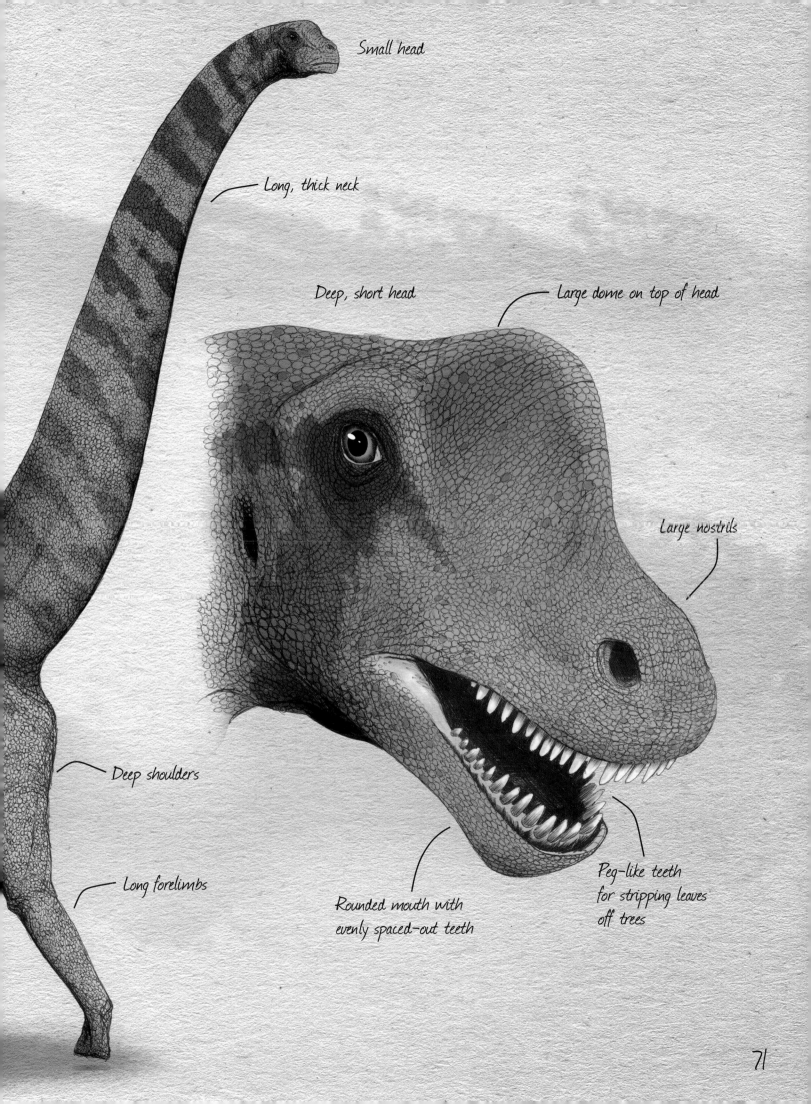

Small head

Long, thick neck

Deep, short head

Large dome on top of head

Large nostrils

Deep shoulders

Long forelimbs

Rounded mouth with
evenly spaced-out teeth

Peg-like teeth
for stripping leaves
off trees

In the shadow of a giant—
a 40-ton adult Giraffatitan
dwarfs the smaller juveniles

A herd of Giraffatitan
travel together, seeking
protection in numbers.
Most individuals are
juveniles weighing
1 ton or more.

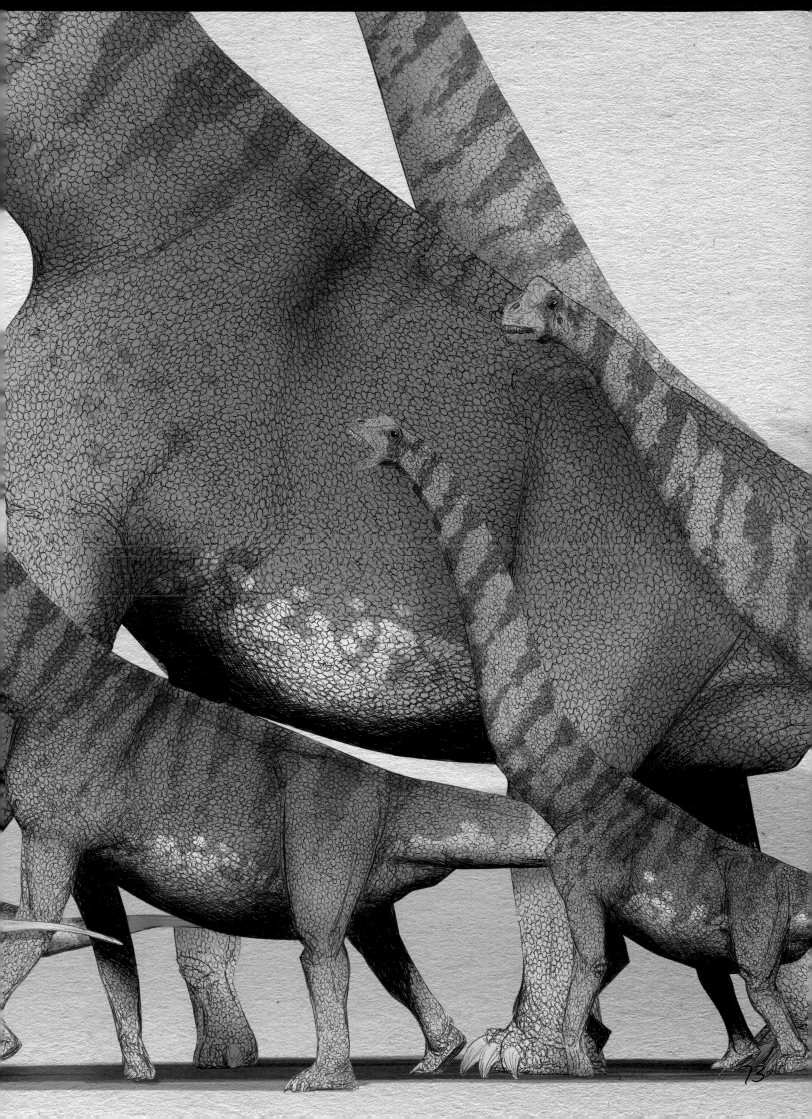

The Ornithischians

It's a foggy morning as the Jurassic sun begins to rise over a field of horsetail plants. As you walk into a field, trees slowly begin to appear through the fog, making themselves more visible with each step you take. There is a drone of insects and mosquitoes in your ear, punctuated by the low grunts and snorting sounds coming from a nearby large animal. The air is thick with humidity and the odor of dung, reminiscent of a farm or petting zoo. The grunting noises continue just ahead of you, as a towering object begins to take shape through the fog. The object moves away from you as it slowly reveals itself—it's an immense dinosaur feeding on the plants beneath it. A cloud of insects forms around its nose and lands on its nostrils. With another deep snort from the dinosaur, the insects disband before reassembling. Its head moves downward as it takes in a mouthful of horsetail plants. Using its hardened beak, it cuts the plants cleanly, then crushes them with its teeth and swallows.

6 feet

3 feet

It is now in plain sight. The unmistakable plates on its back tell you it's a Stegosaurus and it's massive—over 12 feet tall and 20 feet long, about the size of a modern-day elephant. As you approach to get a closer look, the Stegosaurus becomes agitated and begins to rear up as if to say "stay away." This behavior is no different than approaching any wild animal that feels threatened. The fog has now almost entirely lifted, and more animals in the field are now visible. You realize that you are standing among dozens of dinosaurs, all grazing on the same pasture of plants. Many species of ornithischian dinosaurs have come together to peacefully feed, as they have many times in the past. This is a typical breakfast in the Late Jurassic.

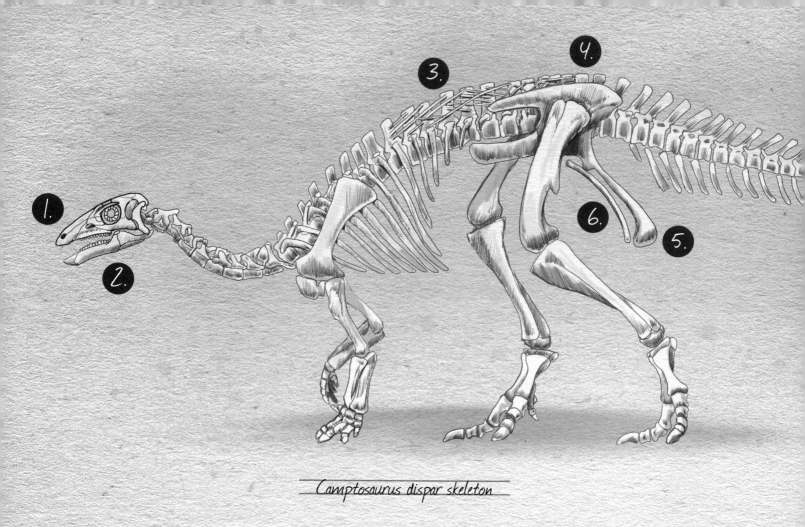

Camptosaurus dispar skeleton

Ornithischians were one of the two major orders of dinosaurs, the other being saurichian (which includes theropods and sauropods). They were known for their hip structure, beaked mouths, and for being herbivores or "plant eaters." Ornithischians were an extremely diverse group, including many different body types and self-defense methods. Even their means of locomotion was diverse: some were bipedal (walking on two legs), others were quadrupedal (walking on four legs), while many were capable of switching between both. If you compare ornithischians to modern-day animals, they would be considered large prey animals, such as horses, cattle, rhinoceroses, and even elephants, as they all had very different body types and means of self-defense, and yet were all herbivorous. Some of the more famous ornithischian dinosaurs include Stegosaurus, Triceratops (Late Cretaceous), Ankylosaurus (Cretaceous), and Hadrosaurs or "duck-billed dinosaurs" (Late Cretaceous).

1. bony beak at front of skull
2. teeth for grinding plant matter
3. bony tendons crisscrossing vertebrae
4. ilium bone is narrow
5. ischium bone faces back
6. pubis bone faces back

Ornithischians of the Late Jurassic

By the Late Jurassic, most ornithischians had clearly developed means by which to confront or escape predators—none more evident than the Stegosaurus stenops and Kentrosaurus aethiopicus. Both dinosaurs had tails clad with sharp, spiked horns and plates rising from their backs. With this deterrent, few, if any, predators were willing to challenge a healthy adult. Kentrosaurus even had 3-foot-long spikes protruding from its shoulders to avoid ambush from the sides. Others like Gargoyleosaurus parkpinorum preferred a passive form of self-defense. Built wide, low to the ground, and armored literally from the nose to the tip of its tail, Gargoyleosaurus made itself a difficult meal to be had. This dinosaur was the ancestor of future dinosaurs from the Cretaceous, like Ankylosaurus, which developed more active forms of self-defense by using a bony growth on the tip of its tail as a club to ward off attackers. Other species like Camptosaurus dispar evolved with larger hind limbs and smaller forelimbs. Because of this, it could outrun many of its predators. When given no means of escape, Camptosaurus was also equipped with a large thumb claw used as a formidable weapon.

Explore the ornithischian dinosaurs in the following pages, and see how they survived the dangers of the Late Jurassic.

Camptosaurus dispar

Location Observed: Wyoming, United States

Family: Camptosauridae

Length: 16 feet (5 meters)

Height: 6 feet (1.8 meters)

Weight: 1,000 pounds

Temperament: Reclusive, shy

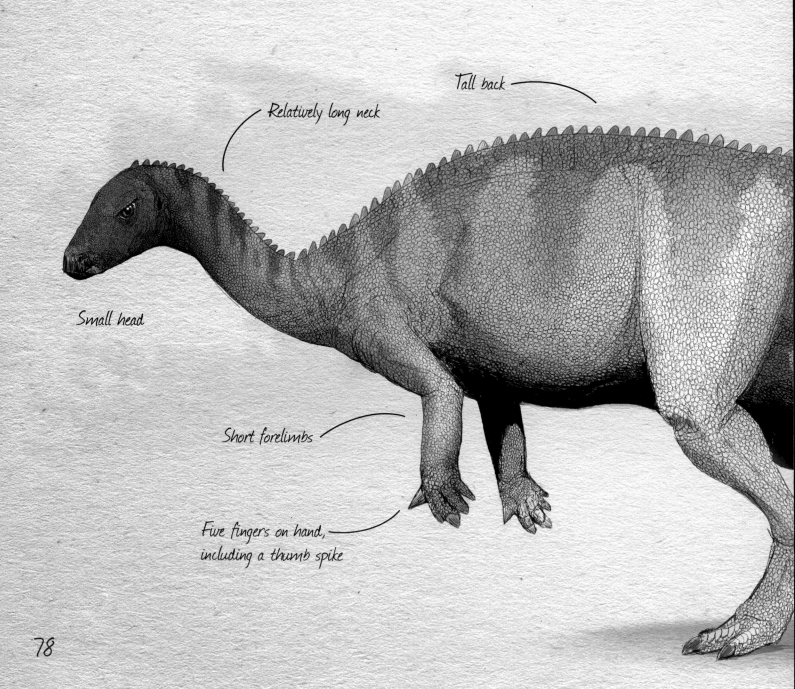

Tall back

Relatively long neck

Small head

Short forelimbs

Five fingers on hand,
including a thumb spike

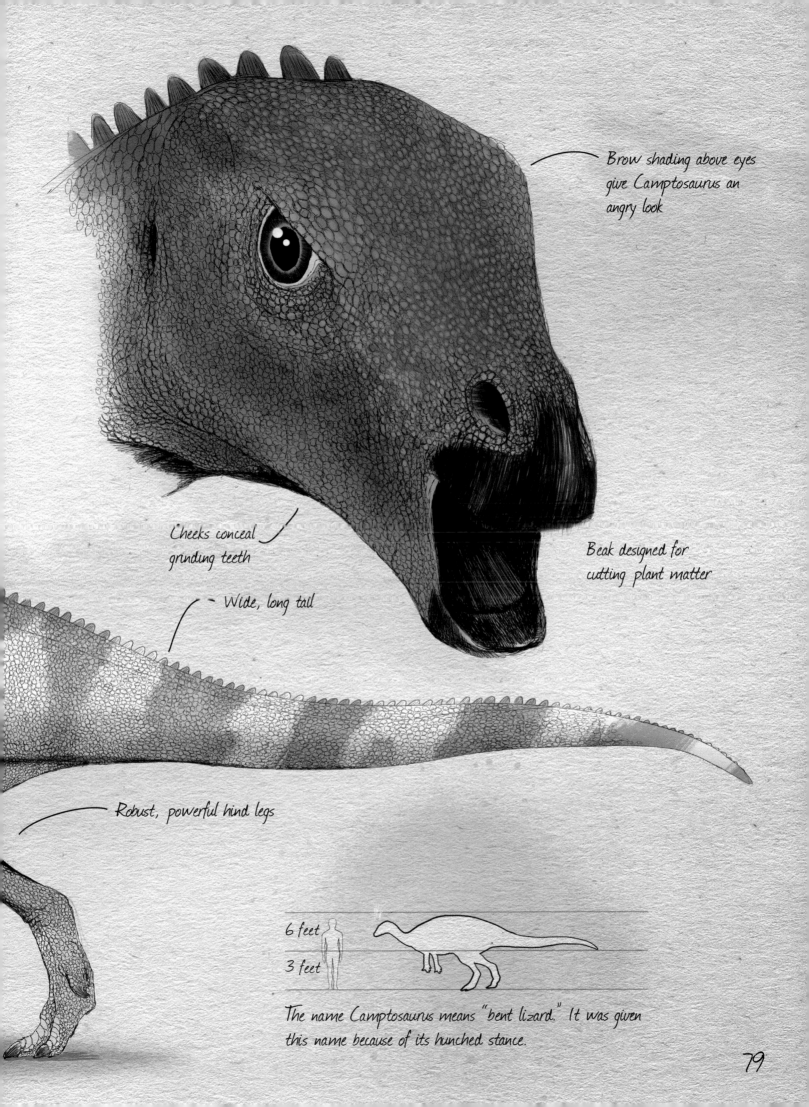

Brow shading above eyes
give Camptosaurus an
angry look

Cheeks conceal
grinding teeth

Beak designed for
cutting plant matter

Wide, long tail

Robust, powerful hind legs

6 feet

3 feet

The name Camptosaurus means "bent lizard." It was given
this name because of its hunched stance.

Very large eyes

Camptosaurus hatchling

Capable of walking on four
legs and running on two to
evade predators

Large thumb spike

Fifth digit is underdeveloped

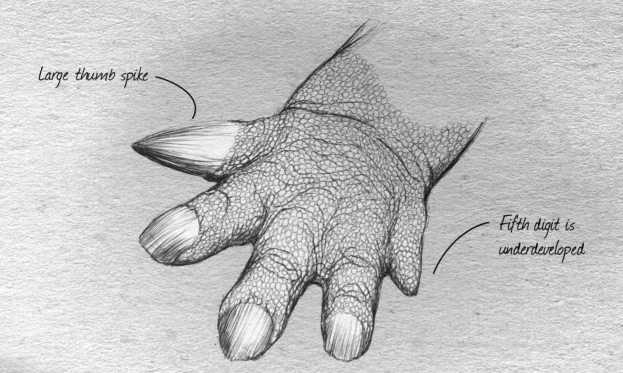

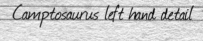
Camptosaurus left hand detail

Always alert for danger—like many modern prey animals, Camptosaurus juveniles gather around a parent for protection

Gargoyleosaurus parkpinorum

Location Observed: Wyoming, United States

Family: Nodosauridae

Length: 9 feet (3 meters)

Height: 3 feet (1 meter)

Weight: 600 pounds

Temperament: Defensive, aggressive

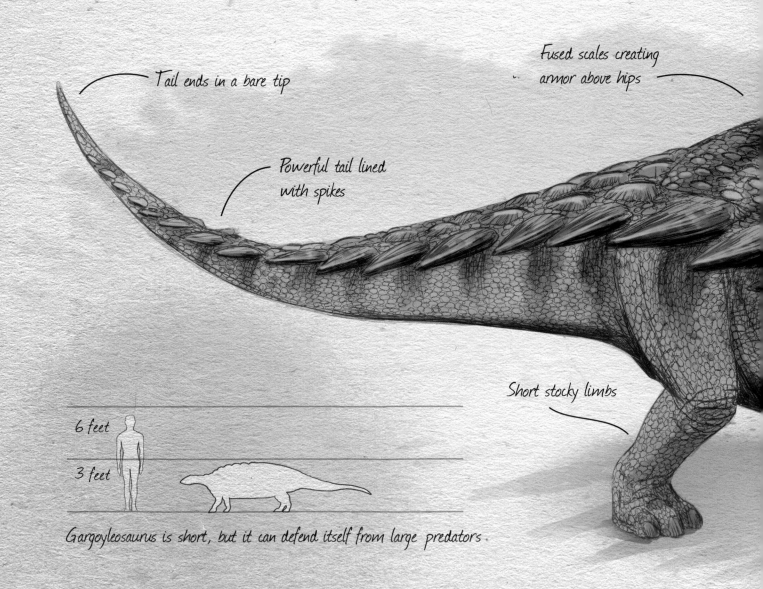

Tail ends in a bare tip

Fused scales creating armor above hips

Powerful tail lined with spikes

Short stocky limbs

6 feet

3 feet

Gargoyleosaurus is short, but it can defend itself from large predators

Fused scales to top
of head

Horns above and below eyes

Small teeth

Triangular-shaped head

Thick scutes form
an armored shell

Long spikes on sides
protect from attack

Sharp bony spikes
line both sides of
the tail

Wielded like an ax,
Gargoyleosaurus' tail is
designed to inflict harm
to any attacker

Dorsal view of Gargoyleosaurus' tail

Its hardened, dome-shaped
carapace is impenetrable

With a wide stance and a low center
of gravity, Gargoyleosaurus is very
difficult to overturn

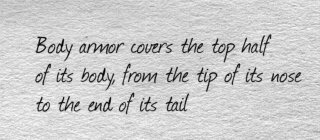

Body armor covers the top half
of its body, from the tip of its nose
to the end of its tail

Long, rectangular head

Beak designed for cutting low-lying plants

Grinding teeth behind cheeks

Seven rows of flat plates along neck and back

Small head

Relatively long neck

Short forelimbs

Enormous spikes protruding from shoulders

Kentrosaurus aethiopicus

Location Observed: Tanzania, Africa

Family: Stegosauridae

Length: 13 feet (4 meters)

Height: 5 feet (1.5 meters)

Weight: 1,500 pounds

Temperament: Defensive, aggressive

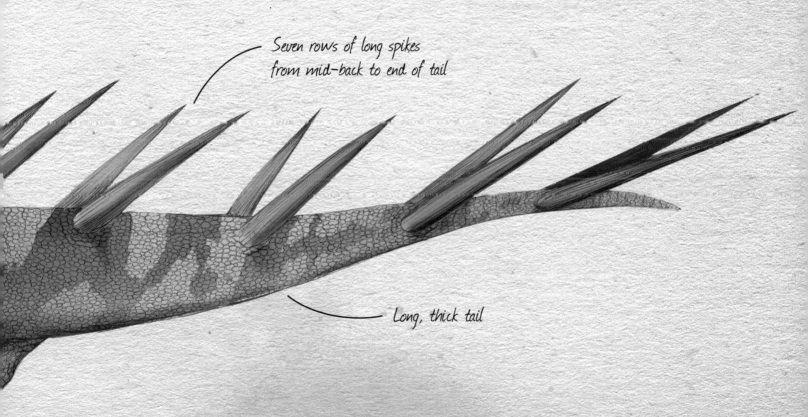

Seven rows of long spikes from mid-back to end of tail

Long, thick tail

Large hind limbs

6 feet

3 feet

Kentrosaurus is much smaller than its American cousin, Stegosaurus

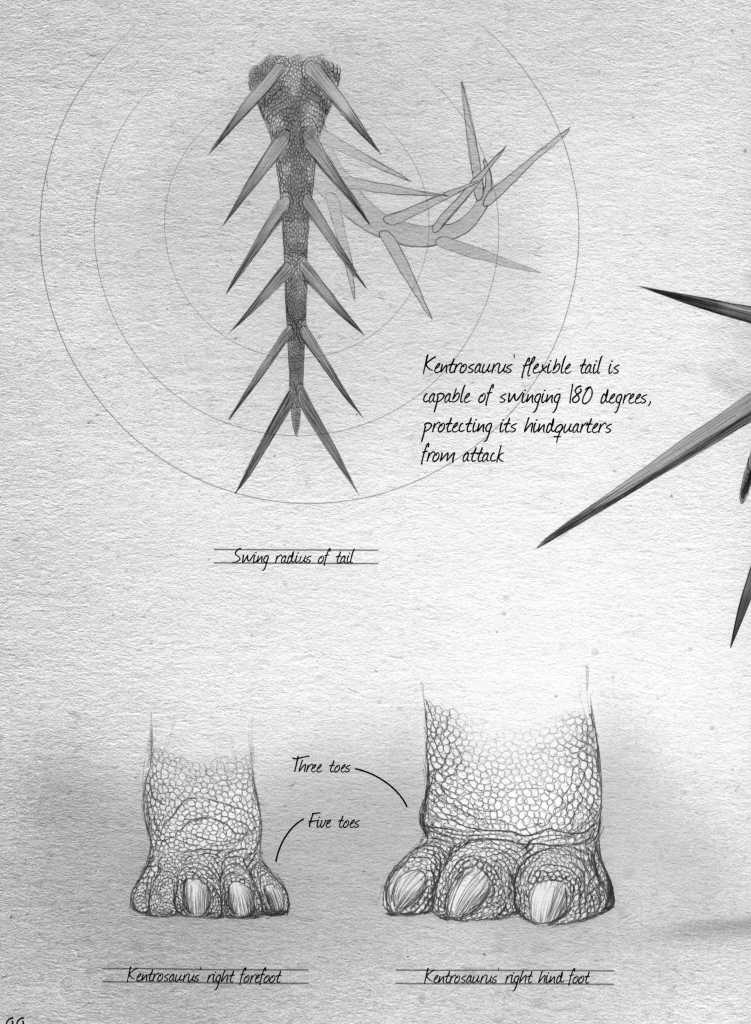

Kentrosaurus' flexible tail is capable of swinging 180 degrees, protecting its hindquarters from attack

Swing radius of tail

Three toes

Five toes

Kentrosaurus' right forefoot

Kentrosaurus' right hind foot

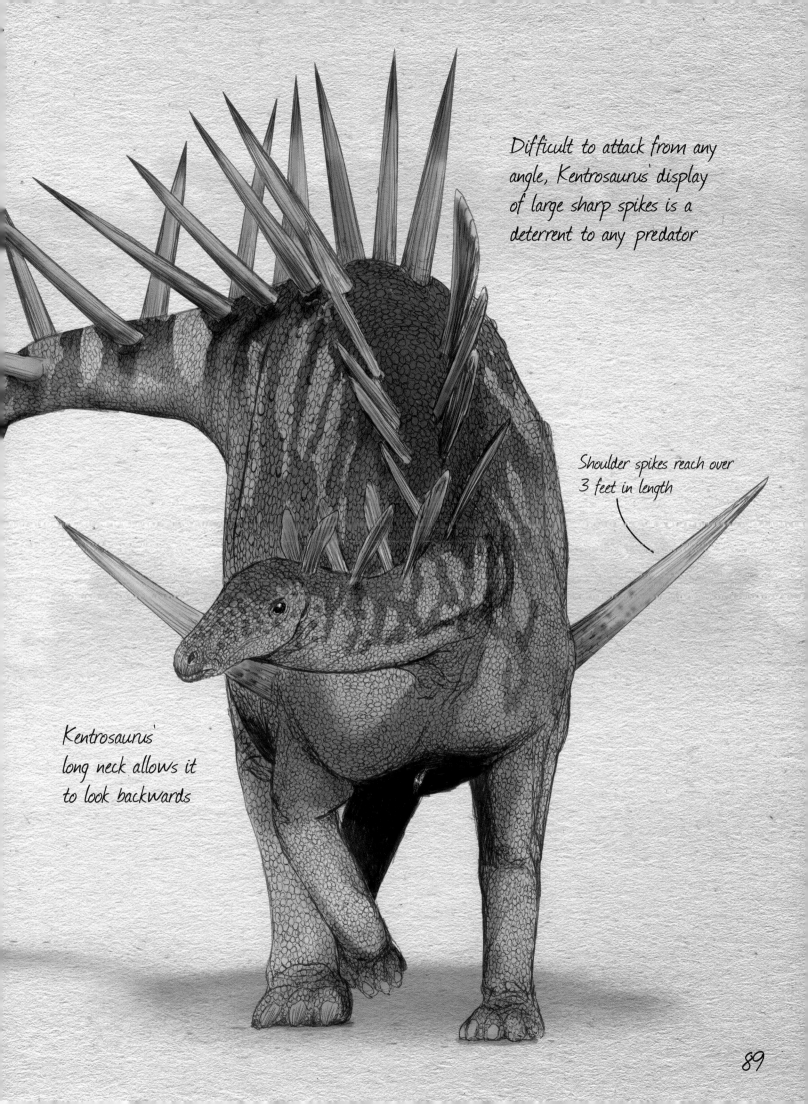

Difficult to attack from any angle, Kentrosaurus' display of large sharp spikes is a deterrent to any predator

Shoulder spikes reach over 3 feet in length

Kentrosaurus' long neck allows it to look backwards

Stegosaurus stenops

Location Observed: Colorado, United States

Family: Stegosauridae

Length: 21 feet (6.5 meters)

Height: 12 feet (3.5 meters)

Weight: 3.5 tons

Temperament: Aggressive

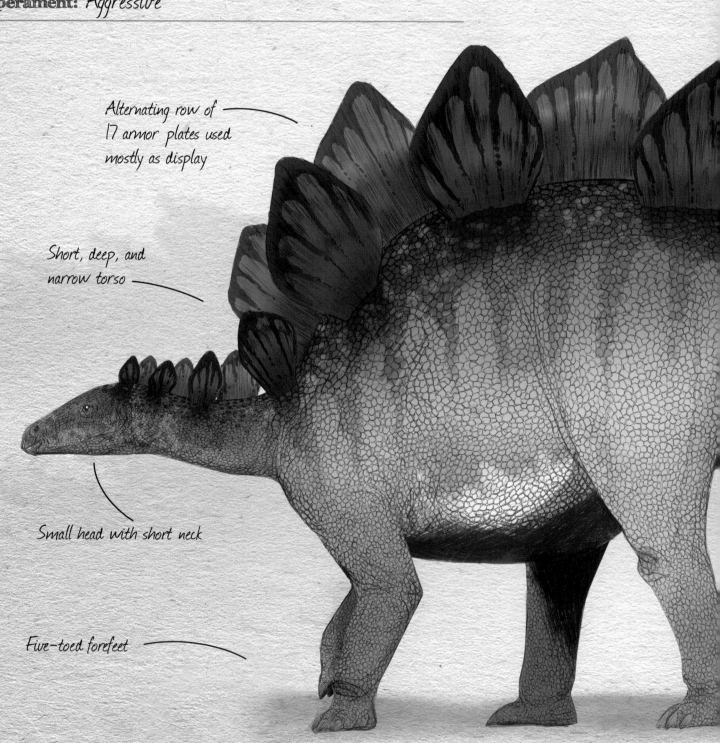

Alternating row of 17 armor plates used mostly as display

Short, deep, and narrow torso

Small head with short neck

Five-toed forefeet

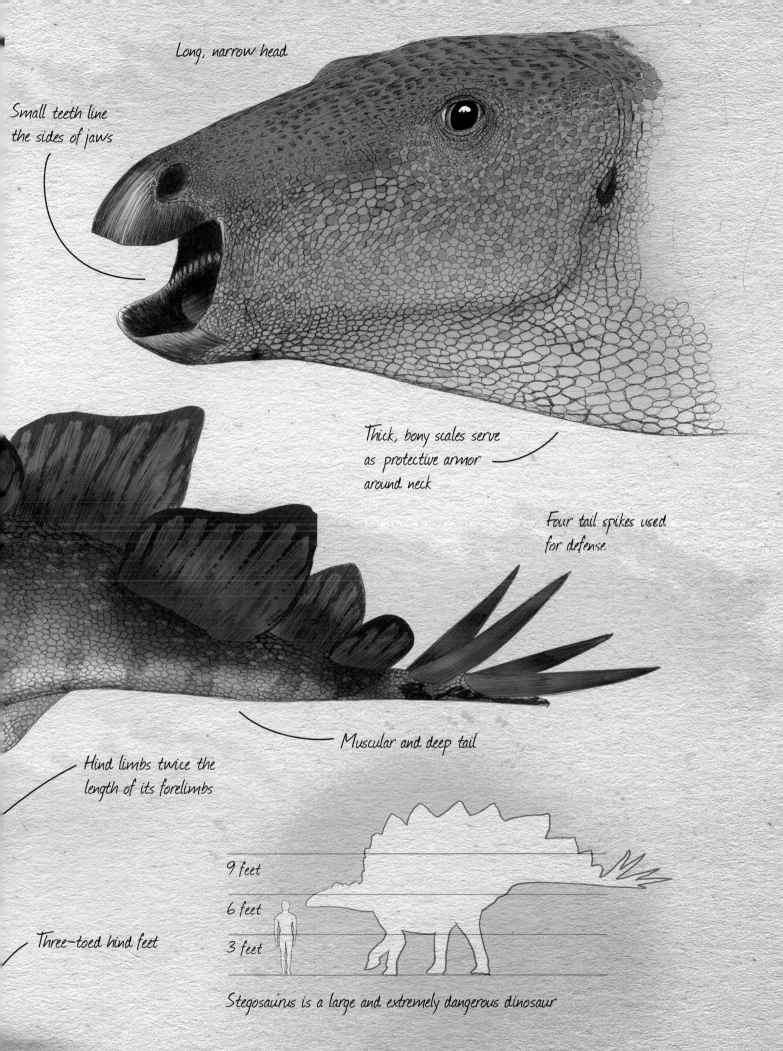

Long, narrow head

Small teeth line
the sides of jaws

Thick, bony scales serve
as protective armor
around neck

Four tail spikes used
for defense.

Muscular and deep tail

Hind limbs twice the
length of its forelimbs

9 feet

6 feet

3 feet

Three-toed hind feet

Stegosaurus is a large and extremely dangerous dinosaur

A healthy, adult
Stegosaurus has
few enemies. Its
size, weight, and
spiked tail make
any predator
think twice.

Rearing up on
two legs makes
Stegosaurus
appear larger
when threatened

Four long tail spikes at
the end of a powerful and
flexible tail can easily kill
any predator

Stegosaurus tail detail

Hatchling and juvenile
Stegosaurus find security and
protection from predators by
staying close to adults

At a couple years old, this
juvenile Stegosaurus reaches
5 feet in length and already
has tail spikes

The Pterosaurs

It's late afternoon, almost dusk, as the sun begins to approach the Jurassic horizon. The evening will be a welcome relief as the sun takes its relentless heat with it as it sets. The day's end signals the arrival of new animals, as well as a new look to the landscape. The last rays of the sun's light accent the millions of insects dotting the air, almost like a cloud. There are mayflies, mosquitoes, damselflies, and dragonflies all moving at different speeds, slowly stirring the cloud they form. With long slashes, larger flying animals begin to cut through the air like a knife. There are dozens of them all feeding on the assortment of insects floating before them. They consist of two body types: one is larger with a pointed beak and tail ending in a diamond-shaped rudder; the other is much smaller with a rounded head.

With effortless precision, they pierce the air and snap up their prey, zigzagging and narrowly missing one another as if they've rehearsed this intricate dance. The largest of them has a wingspan about the size of an eagle, while the smallest species is no bigger than a blue jay. One swoops inches from your head as you feel the wind rush past you and hear the quick flapping of its wings. You are an eyewitness to the daily feast of the pterosaurs: the absolute masters of flight during the Late Jurassic.

Pterosaurs, which means "winged reptile" in ancient Greek, were the first vertebrates to evolve self-sufficient flight millions of years before mammals (bats) or even birds.

They flew using the same principles modern birds use today, with wings made from a fibrous membrane extending from their elongated fourth fingers and attached to their hind limbs. Pterosaurs' anatomy was designed to be very efficient for flight. Its skeleton included a system of air sacs that worked with the lungs to aid in respiration and reduce body weight. Pterosaur skeletons were constructed of a strong framework of hollow bones, with skulls containing openings called "fenestra" to help reduce weight without sacrificing structural support. They were truly a masterpiece of engineering.

Pterosaurs of the Late Jurassic

By the Late Jurassic, pterosaurs had evolved specialized adaptations for hunting and flight. Species like Rhamphorhynchus muensteri were equipped with thin, forward-facing teeth designed to spear insects and fish in mid-flight. Its curved beak also had sharpened tips on both the skull and jaw to ensure prey didn't escape. Rhamphorhynchus was also known for its long, rigid tail, which it used as a counterbalance, much like the tail of a kite. By swinging its tail, it could change direction and control its flight at will. Anurognathus ammoni, by comparison, flew without the aid of a long tail for balance. Its long, slender wings and rounded frog-like face were more suited for flying in tighter quarters between trees and obstacles where it too hunted for insects in midair. Anurognathus also had large, evolved eyes to allow for vision in low-light conditions, making it an excellent nocturnal hunter.

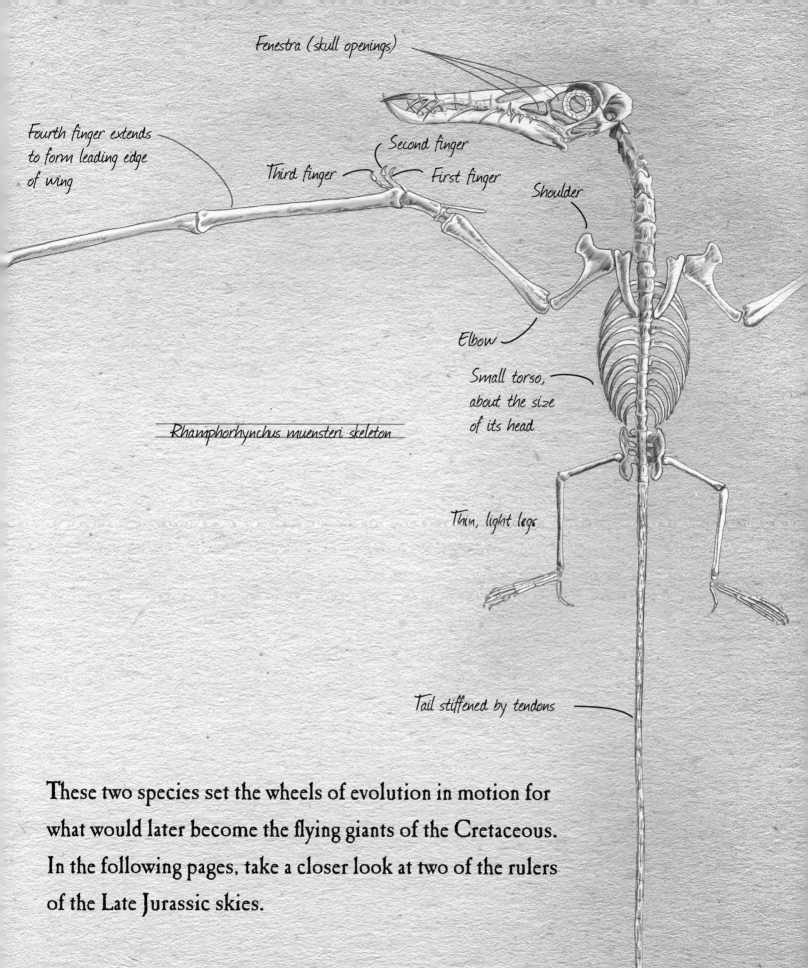

Fenestra (skull openings)

Fourth finger extends
to form leading edge
of wing

Second finger

Third finger

First finger

Shoulder

Elbow

Rhamphorhynchus muensteri skeleton

Small torso,
about the size
of its head

Thin, light legs

Tail stiffened by tendons

These two species set the wheels of evolution in motion for
what would later become the flying giants of the Cretaceous.
In the following pages, take a closer look at two of the rulers
of the Late Jurassic skies.

Anurognathus ammoni

Location Observed: Germany

Family: Anurognathidae

Length: 6 inches (.15 meter)

Height: 20 inches (.5 meter) wingspan

Weight: 5 grams

Temperament: Elusive

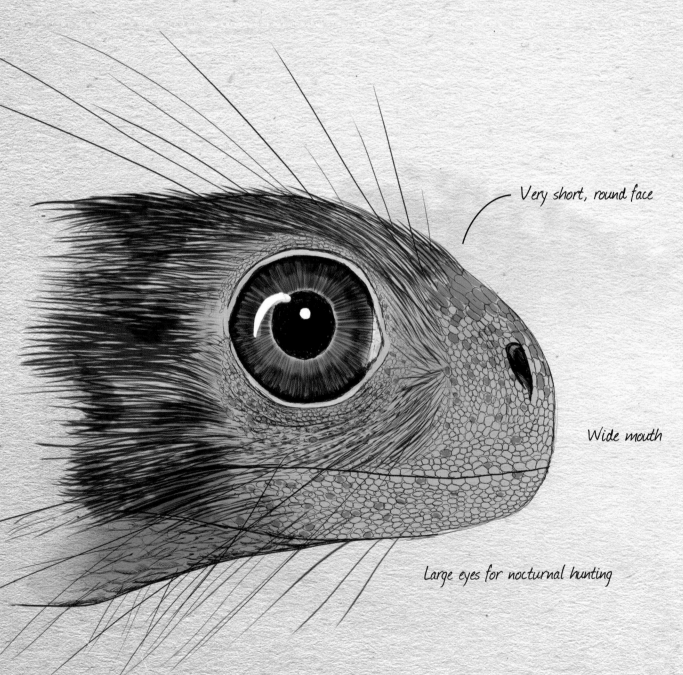

Very short, round face

Wide mouth

Large eyes for nocturnal hunting

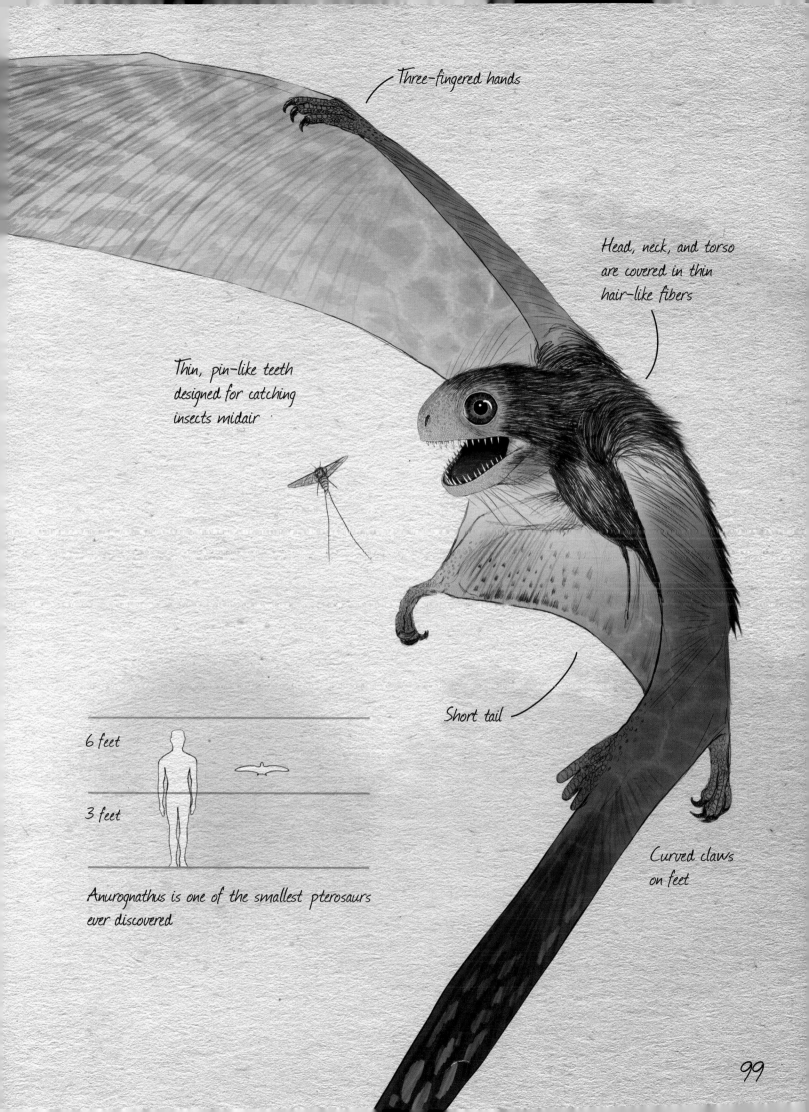

Three-fingered hands

Head, neck, and torso are covered in thin hair-like fibers

Thin, pin-like teeth designed for catching insects midair

Short tail

Curved claws on feet

6 feet

3 feet

Anurognathus is one of the smallest pterosaurs ever discovered

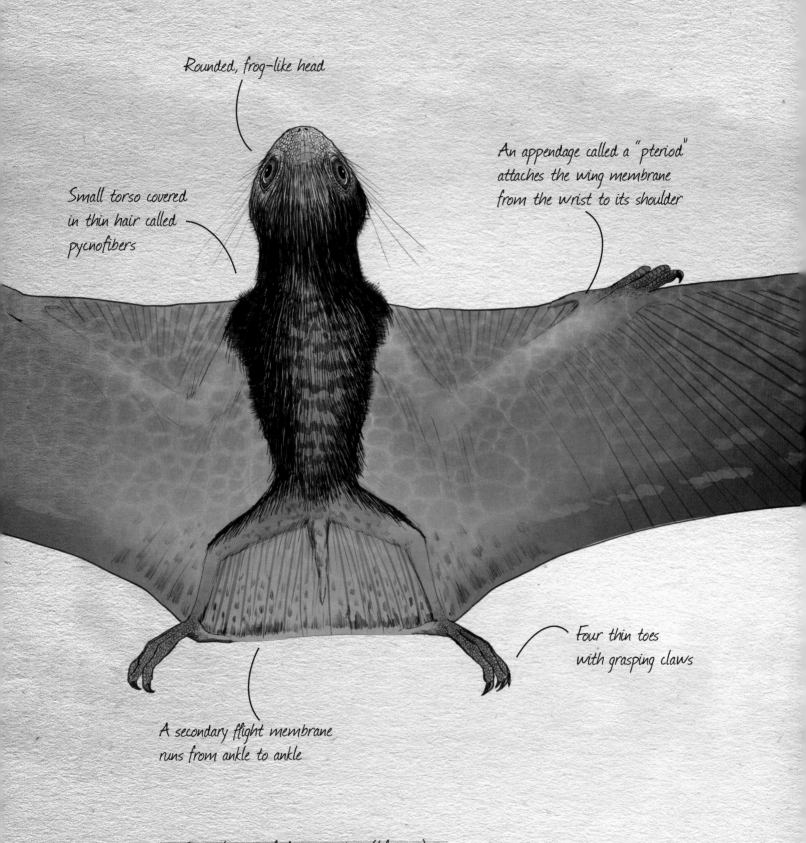

Rounded, frog-like head

An appendage called a "pteriod" attaches the wing membrane from the wrist to its shoulder

Small torso covered in thin hair called pycnofibers

Four thin toes with grasping claws

A secondary flight membrane runs from ankle to ankle

Dorsal view of Anurognathus (life size)

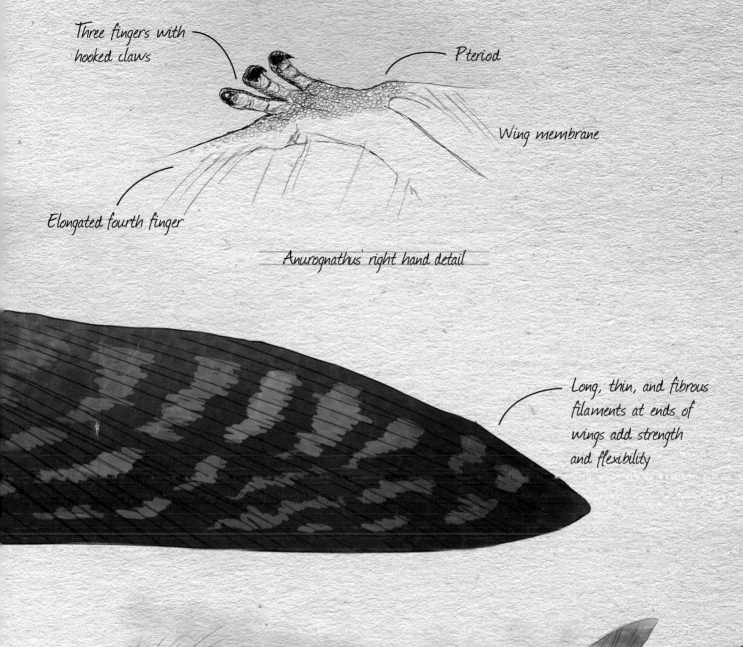

Three fingers with hooked claws

Pteriod

Wing membrane

Elongated fourth finger

Anurognathus' right hand detail

Long, thin, and fibrous filaments at ends of wings add strength and flexibility

Using its strong muscles, Anurognathus launches itself into the air by leaping forward and pushing off with its forelimbs

Rhamphorhynchus muensteri

Location Observed: *Germany*

Family: *Rhamphorhynchidae*

Length: *4 feet (1.26 meters)*

Height: *5 feet, 9 inches (1.81 meters) wingspan*

Weight: *2.5 pounds*

Temperament: *Reclusive, shy*

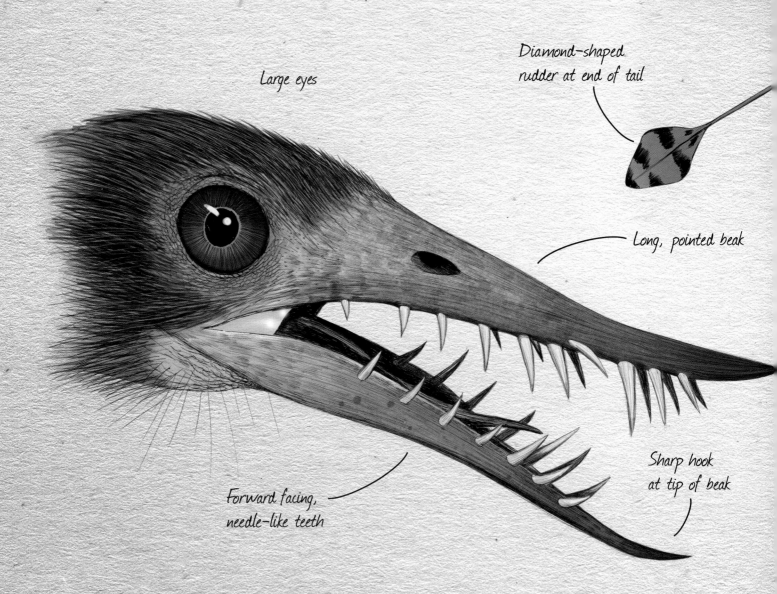

Large eyes

Diamond-shaped rudder at end of tail

Long, pointed beak

Forward facing, needle-like teeth

Sharp hook at tip of beak

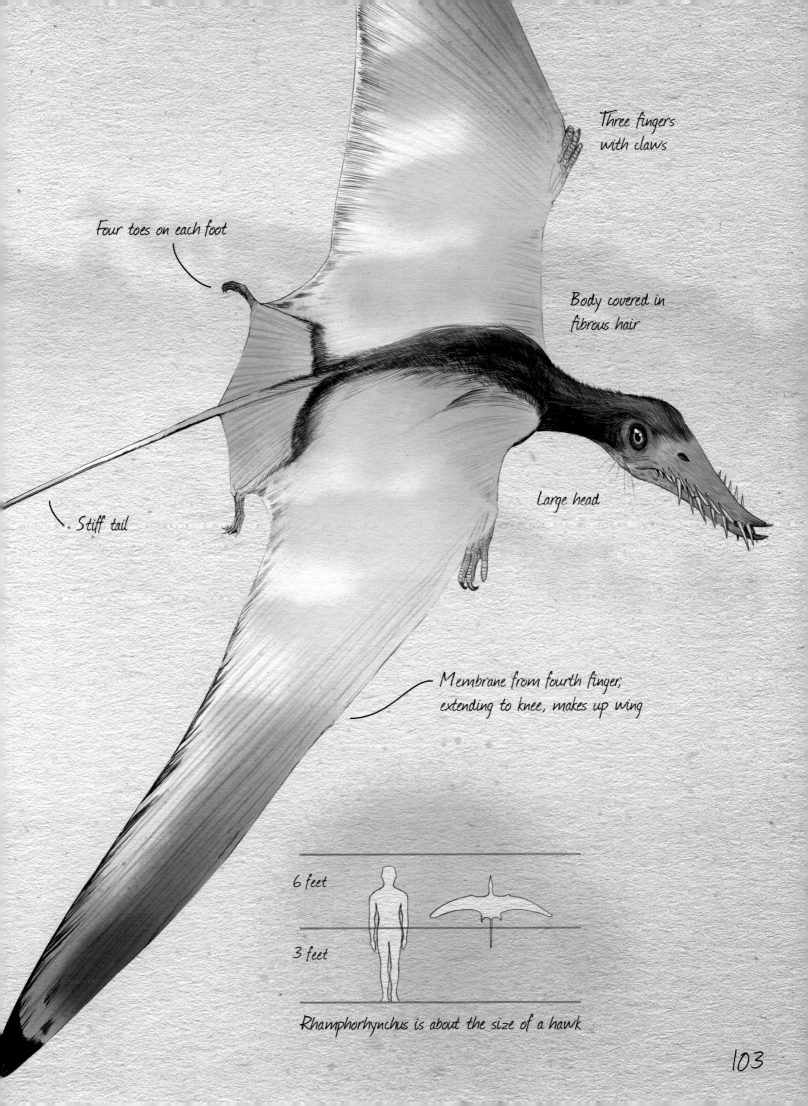

Three fingers
with claws

Four toes on each foot

Body covered in
fibrous hair

Stiff tail

Large head

Membrane from fourth finger,
extending to knee, makes up wing

6 feet

3 feet

Rhamphorhynchus is about the size of a hawk

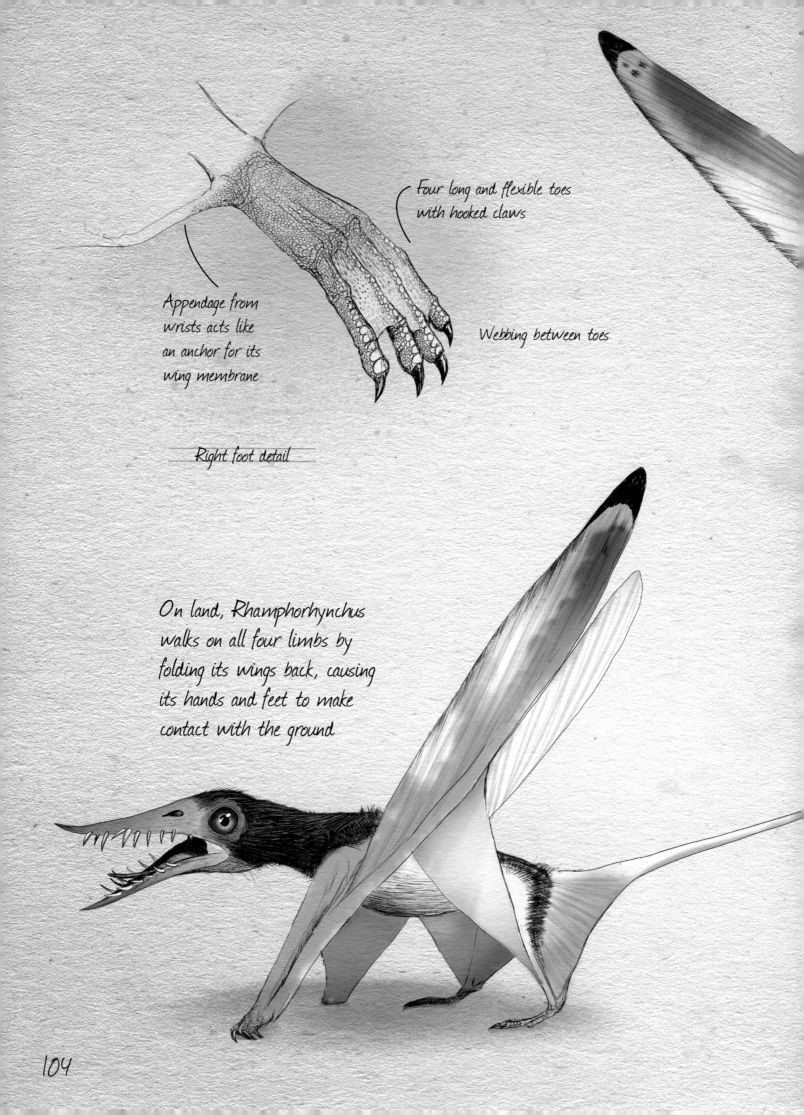

Four long and flexible toes with hooked claws

Appendage from wrists acts like an anchor for its wing membrane

Webbing between toes

Right foot detail

On land, Rhamphorhynchus walks on all four limbs by folding its wings back, causing its hands and feet to make contact with the ground

Opportunistic in nature, no
catch goes unchallenged

Rhamphorhynchus feeds mostly
on fish, but is also known to
eat small flying insects

By spreading its legs,
Rhamphorhynchus creates
a broad surface area
for its wings

Rhamphorhynchus' long, rigid
tail acts like a counterbalance,
allowing it to effortlessly change
direction midair

The Mammals

It's another typical day in the Late Jurassic, hot and steamy with the constant harassment of biting insects. You escape into the shade of a grove to avoid the sun, and you are surprised to see the trees alive with movement. Jumping from branch to branch, there are several small animals with long tails interacting playfully. They look like a mixture of a squirrel and an opossum and act very much like modern-day mammals. They have total command of the trees where they feel at home, oblivious to any of the dangers that come with living on the ground. These animals are a startling contrast to the other wildlife experienced in the Jurassic. Watching them almost makes you forget you are 150 million years away from the earth you know. These are the early mammals, your great ancestors, and a glimpse of what evolution has in store for the earth.

The first true mammals began to appear around the Late Triassic period, about 50 to 75 million years before the Late Jurassic. They evolved alongside the dinosaurs, but remained small, carving out evolutionary niches and not competing directly with them. Their small size was a blessing in disguise, as it allowed them to survive past the extinction

event that killed off the dinosaurs around 65 million years ago. Afterwards, the mammals would flourish and slowly begin to evolve into larger species, giving rise to early primates and ultimately humans.

Mammals of the Late Jurassic

By the Late Jurassic, mammals adapted to different lifestyles, including species like Fruitafossor windscheffeli, who developed specialized traits designed for digging and eating termites and ants. Others like Castorocauda lutrasimilis made the water their home by evolving the attributes necessary for a semi-aquatic life, one similar to a modern-day otter.

In this section, we will take a look at two well-documented species: Shenshou lui, an arboreal or "tree-dwelling" animal from China, and Juramaia sinensis, whose name means "Jurassic Mother," also from China. Shenshou evolved hands and feet with opposable fingers perfect for grasping branches and a prehensile tail capable of gripping onto trees and acting like a fifth limb. Juramaia is equally at home in the trees as on the ground and is built more like a small mouse or shrew. What makes Juramaia more notable is that it is considered to be the first placental mammal, meaning it gave birth to live young which developed in a womb. These are two of the early mammals who lived among dinosaurs and foreshadow the evolutionary changes the earth is soon to experience.

Shenshou lui

Location Observed: Liaoning, China

Family: Mammalia

Length: 1 foot (.3 meter)

Weight: 10 ounces

Temperament: Cautious

Large eyes allow Shenshou to see in low-light conditions

Very large incisors

6 feet

3 feet

Shenshou is about the size of a squirrel

Shenshou live almost exclusively in trees and are omnivorous, eating insects, nuts, and fruit

Shenshou's hands show a thumb adapted for grasping branches

Long, prehensile tail

Juramaia sinensis

Location Observed: Liaoning, China

Family: Mammalia

Length: 5 inches (.12 meter)

Weight: 15 grams

Temperament: Reclusive, shy

Long tail covered in hair

Feet designed for both climbing and running on the ground

3 feet

18 inches

Juramaia is about the size of a shrew

Long, conical teeth
used for catching and eating
insects and worms

Body covered in
short hair

Long snout

Juramaia head detail

Pronunciation Key

Theropods (Theer-uh-pods)
Allosaurus fragilis (Al-oh-sore-us, fraj-ill-iss)
Archaeopteryx lithographica (Are-key-op-trex, lith-o-graf-e-ka)
Ceratosaurus nasicornis (Sir-at-toe-sore-us, nay-si-corn-iss)
Compsognathus longipes (Comp-sog-nay-thus, long-gipes)
Guanlong wucaii (Ga-wan-long, goo-kai)
Ornitholestes hermanni (Or-nith-oh-less-teaze, her-man-knee)
Torvosaurus tanneri (Tor-vo-sore-us, tan-nery)
Yangchuanosaurus shangyouensis (Yan-chwahn-oh-sore-us, shang-u-en-sis)
Yi qi (Ee-chee)

Sauropods (Sore-uh-pods)
Brontosaurus louisae (Bron-toe-sore-us, louise-ay)
Camarasaurus supremus (Kam-ara-sore-us, sue-preme-us)
Diplodocus hallorum (Di-plod-oh-kus, hall-ore-um)
Giraffatitan brancai (Ji-raf-a-tie-tan, bran-kai)

Ornithischians (Ore-ni-thisk-key-ahns)
Camptosaurus dispar (Kamp-toe-sore-us, dis-par)
Gargoyleosaurus parkpinorum (Gar-goy-lo-sore-us, park-pin-ore-um)
Kentrosaurus aethiopicus (Ken-tro-sore-us, ethi-opee-cus)
Stegosaurus stenops (Steg-go-sore-us, sten-opps)

Pterosaurs (Ter-uh-sore)
Anurognathus ammoni (An-your-og-nath-us, am-mon-i)
Rhamphorhynchus muensteri (Ram-for-ink-uss, moon-stery)

Mammals
Shenshou lui (Shen-shoe, le-oh)
Juramaia sinensis (Joor-ah-my-ah, sin-n-sis)

About the Authors

Juan Carlos Alonso

Juan Carlos Alonso (author and illustrator) is a Cuban American graphic designer, creative director, illustrator, and author of the award-winning *Ancient Earth Journal* series. He has over 30 years experience in the graphic design/illustration field. In 1992 he founded Alonso & Company, a creative boutique specializing in branding, design, and advertising. His passion for nature has taken him around the world, from Australia to the Galapagos Islands, to study animals. Along with his work in the graphic arts, he is also an accomplished wildlife sculptor, focusing mostly on prehistoric animals.

Gregory S. Paul

Gregory S. Paul (co-author) is an American freelance researcher, author, and illustrator who works in paleontology. He is best known for his work and research on theropod dinosaurs and his detailed illustrations, both live and skeletal. Professionally investigating and restoring dinosaurs for three decades, Paul received an on-screen credit as a dinosaur specialist on *Jurassic Park* and Discovery Channel's *When Dinosaurs Roamed America* and *Dinosaur Planet*. He is the author and illustrator of *Predatory Dinosaurs of the World* (1988), *The Complete Illustrated Guide to Dinosaur Skeletons* (1996), *Dinosaurs of the Air* (2001), *The Princeton Field Guide To Dinosaurs* (2010), *Gregory S. Paul's Dinosaur Coffee Table Book* (2010), editor of *The Scientific American Book of Dinosaurs* (2000), and co-author of the award-winning *Ancient Earth Journal* series. Paul has named over twelve prehistoric animal species and has had two dinosaur species named after him (*Cryptovolans pauli* and *Sellacoxa pauli*) based on his innovative theories.

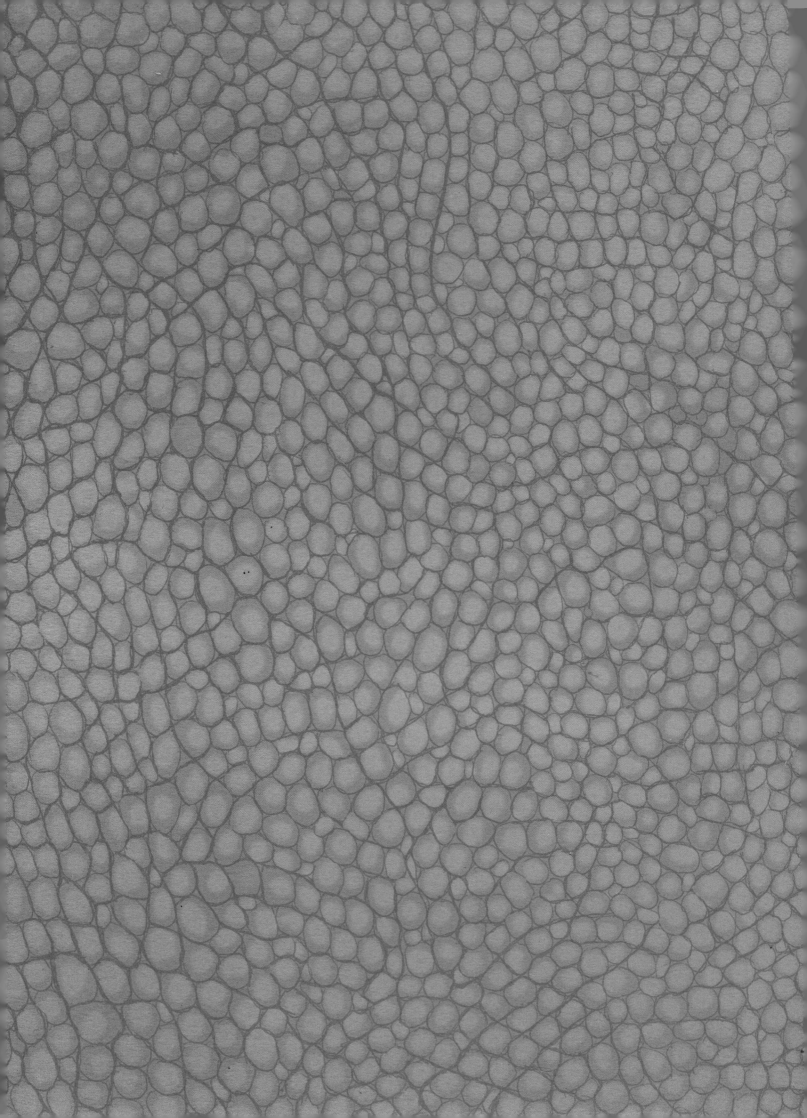